SHAYTAN AND THE NAFS

OVERCOMING OUR STRONGEST ENEMIES

UMM MUHAMMAD ABIZER

ISBN:

Paperback: 978-9948-19-293-0

Title: Shaytān or The Nafs: Overcoming our Strongest Enemies

Second Edition

Editors:
Development Editing - Hend Hegazi
Copy Line Editing - Umm Marwan Ebrahim
Proofreading - Sarah Adam, Anna Barawi

Cover Design by Khalid Barawi

Instagram & Facebook:
@thabaatpublications

Email: thabaatpublications@gmail.com

Approved by nmc.gov.ae
Application number MC-01-01-3082047

Typeset & Printed at A1 Grafix Studio

+91-9819189965 a1grafixstudio@gmail.com

Contents

PREFACE

بسم الله الرحمن الرحيم

All thanks and praises are due to Allah alone. The One, the Almighty, the All-Merciful. May His blessings and peace be upon Prophet Muhammad (ﷺ), the last of His Messengers and Prophets; his family; his Companions; and all those who follow in his footsteps until the end of time.

The very thought of an enemy triggers in us a sense of discomfort, uneasiness, depression, fear, anxiety, hostility, resentfulness, and/or anger.

This is because it is associated with someone:

- who hates us
- tricks and deceives us
- wants our downfall
- threatens us
- tries to harm or even attack us and cause our destruction

...in fact, someone who is actively working against us.

Because of the innate harm an enemy is capable of afflicting on us, Allah instructs us in the Quran to take precautions against the enemy and not to wait until they attack. We are told to be prepared and be on alert for their assault at all times.

"And prepare against them whatever you can of power and of horses, to frighten thereby the enemy of Allah, and your enemy, and others besides them, whom you do not know (but) Allah knows. And whatever things you spend in the way of Allah shall be repaid to you in full, and you will not be dealt with unjustly."
(Sūrah al-Anfāl, 8:60)

The concept of this verse and its application is vast and universal. The admonitions it contains are not limited to our mortal enemies.

Just as we prepare for any struggle against enemies that we can see, we must also gather all necessary forces to fight our unseen enemies: Shaytān and our nafs. We need to be aware that the consequences of their harmful attacks are not limited to our temporary, worldly life. Rather, they extend to our eternal life in the Hereafter, threatening our entry into Jannah. They are our greatest stumbling blocks to eternal prosperity.

Allah has warned us against following Shaytān and commanded us to oppose him. He says:

"Surely Shaytān is an enemy to you, so treat him as an enemy. He only invites his followers that they may become the dwellers of the blazing Fire."
(Sūrah Fātir, 35:6)

Ibn al-Qayyim (ﷺ) said:

"Beware of enabling Shaytān to establish himself in the very home of your thoughts and intentions, as he will corrupt them in such a manner that will make difficult its correction thereafter. He will cast all sort of whisperings and harmful thoughts at you and he will

prevent you from thinking about what may benefit you. (In that case) it is you who have aided him against yourself by empowering him over your heart and thoughts, and he then placed you in the possession of such thoughts." (Al-Fawā'id)

Such is the danger arising from Shaytān.

Regarding the nafs, scholars have described fighting against the desires of the nafs as similar to climbing a mountain. It is not an easy journey. If we fail to exercise control over our nafs, it will lead us to heedlessly commit sins, like backbiting, casting lustful glances, breaking ties with next of kin, watching movies, and so on, thereby tainting our eemān.

Regarding the weight of eemān, Ibn al-Qayyim (ﷺ) said:

"Eemān is a reason for bringing about every good; and every good in the life of this world and the Hereafter—its factor is eemān. Likewise, every evil in the life of this world and the Hereafter—its reason is an absence of eemān." (Fath al-Bārī)

While we acknowledge that both Shaytān and the nafs firmly pursue our devastation and ruin, several questions arise:

- Which of the two is more dangerous?
- Whose attack is stronger?
- Whom should we strive more vigorously against to thwart?

Getting answers to these questions are vital so as to choose the appropriate mechanisms to tackle and conquer these two enemies. We cannot afford to lead a life of heedlessness, as they are both waiting for a chance to get the better of us.

Alhamdulillāh, Allah Almighty has not left us unaided. He has given us the perfect guidance concerning the nuances of how to tackle Shaytān and the nafs.

Read on to:

- Discover the reality of Shaytān and the nafs

- Find the answers to the above questions

- Discover the guidelines to overpower Shaytān and the nafs, the greatest obstacles to achieving our ultimate goal of attaining the pleasure of Allah

Every time we take a step towards Allah, Shaytān and the nafs intend to cut off our path to Him. Sometimes we may feel weak as we try to scale the tests and trials that we face in our lives. Sometimes we may get discouraged and even consider giving up. Hold on and remember Allah in those times.

One of the five things that Allah commanded Yahya (عليه السلام) to enjoin upon the Children of Israel was: "I command you to remember Allah, for this is like a man who is being pursued by the enemy, then he comes to a strong fortress and saves himself from them. Similarly, a man cannot save himself from his enemy except by means of remembering Allah." (Sunan at-Tirmidhī)

All thanks and praises are due to Allah, exalted be He, the Most High, for providing me with an opportunity to write this guide. I would like to acknowledge everyone who helped me in creating this book, and express special thanks to my teachers, whose lectures helped me attain the solutions mentioned in this book. May Allah make it a source of sadaqah jāriyah (continuous benefit till the end of time) for all of them. āmīn.

Chapter 1

Shaytān: The Open Enemy

وَقُل رَّبِّ أَعُوذُ بِكَ مِنْ هَمَزَٰتِ ٱلشَّيَٰطِينِ ﴿٩٧﴾
وَأَعُوذُ بِكَ رَبِّ أَن يَحْضُرُونِ ﴿٩٨﴾

My Lord! I seek refuge with You from
the whisperings of the Shayātīn (devils).
And I seek refuge with You, my Lord,
lest they may attend (or come near) me.
(Sūrah al-Mu'minūn, 23:97-98)

Imagine someone who became our enemy even before we were born, whose only aim is to take us to Hell with him. An enemy we can't even see. Tackling and combating an enemy that we can see is a challenging and stressful task in itself. Then, imagine tackling an unseen enemy. How much more difficult and dangerous would that be!

Such is Shaytān, whom Allah Almighty Himself declares as our open enemy, warning us against following him. He, the Glorified, says:

أَلَمْ أَعْهَدْ إِلَيْكُمْ يَٰبَنِىٓ ءَادَمَ أَن لَّا تَعْبُدُوا۟ ٱلشَّيْطَٰنَ ۖ إِنَّهُۥ لَكُمْ عَدُوٌّ مُّبِينٌ ﴿٦٠﴾

"Did I not ordain for you, oh Children of Adam, that you should not follow Shaytān. (For) verily, he is a plain enemy to you."
(Sūrah Yā-Sīn, 36:60)

The word Shaytān comes from the root word 'shathana' which means 'to be far away from something'. Shaytān is far away from any goodness and far away from the mercy of Allah, the Almighty.

He hates mankind, the Children of Adam (عليه السلام). He is hostile against them because he was cursed and banished from the mercy of Allah as a result of his refusal to obey Allah's command to prostrate to Adam (عليه السلام).

قَالَ فَٱخۡرُجۡ مِنۡهَا فَإِنَّكَ رَجِيمٞ ٧٧ وَإِنَّ عَلَيۡكَ لَعۡنَتِيٓ إِلَىٰ يَوۡمِ ٱلدِّينِ ٧٨

"Then get out from here. For verily, you are outcast. And verily, My curse is on you till the Day of Recompense." (Sūrah Sād, 38:77-78)

He then asked Allah to grant him respite until the Day of Resurrection, and He Almighty granted him that:

قَالَ أَنظِرۡنِيٓ إِلَىٰ يَوۡمِ يُبۡعَثُونَ ١٤ قَالَ إِنَّكَ مِنَ ٱلۡمُنظَرِينَ ١٥

"(Iblīs) said: 'Allow me respite till the Day they are raised up [i.e., the Day of Resurrection].' (Allah) said: 'You are of those respited.'" (Sūrah al-'Araf , 7:14-15)

Instead of regretting and asking Allah for forgiveness, Shaytān rebelled and transgressed further. Out of his jealousy towards us, he vowed:

... وَلَأُضِلَّنَّهُمۡ

"I will surely lead them astray... " (Sūrah an-Nisā', 4:119)

This verse shows Shaytān's strong determination to plot against us. He is extremely treacherous and he lies in wait for us on the Straight Path. He comes to us from every side and in every way. He is always alert, on guard, and insistent on leading us astray.

Indeed, he is living up to his covenant to mislead us. Look at the majority of humanity today; many amongst us are confused and in doubt regarding the true path to salvation.

Furthermore, Shaytān promised to tempt us with false desires, thus deluding us with false aspirations of this world.

.. وَلَأُمَنِّيَنَّهُمْ

"...and I will (surely) give them false passions and desires... "
(Sūrah an-Nisā', 4:119)

For most of us, Shaytān has succeeded in making this worldly life our ultimate purpose. By tempting us with the attractions of this temporary life, he has kept us so busy that we don't even have time to think about our true purpose, i.e., the worship and pleasure of Allah. He distracts us by enticing us to spend excessive amounts of time watching television or scrolling through the internet and social media. He can turn seemingly innocent acts, like online shopping for example, into obsessions, overwhelming us in the cares of this world and ripping us further and further away from our connection with Allah.

Through his whispers, Shaytān beautifies sins, tempting us towards harām and evil acts. He enjoins these vile behaviors, and, unfortunately, many people fall prey to his deceptions.

Disobedience of one command led to Shaytān's humiliation and destruction. Think about how many commands of Allah we disobey and still feel secure from His punishment. May Allah protect us.

1.1 The Nature of the whispers of Shaytān

The Messenger of Allah (ﷺ) said:
"The Shaytān flows in a man like his blood."
(Sahīh Muslim)

Shaytān steers through us like flowing blood. He therefore knows our weaknesses, and whispers his evil suggestions accordingly, beautifying the pathway to sins. He misses no chance to cause us harm and destruction.

ٱلَّذِى يُوَسْوِسُ فِى صُدُورِ ٱلنَّاسِ ﴿٥﴾

" ... who whispers in the breasts of mankind"
(Sūrah an-Nās, 114:5)

The method of his whispers is very subtle, like a feel-good breeze that softly brushes the leaves of trees without causing them any disturbance. His whispers, though gentle, are continuous. He never gives up. Whether we are alone or in public, during the day or at night, while we are heedless of his mischief, he spares no opportunity to mislead us from the Straight Path.

Shaytān is a strong external force that causes our eemān to decrease. Because of his intense enmity towards us, he has no desire or goal other than to weaken and corrupt us. Whoever submits to the whisperings of Shaytān, complies with his ideas, and does not retreat to Allah for refuge from him, his eemān will gradually diminish and may eventually disappear entirely.

It is for this reason that Allah warns us of Shaytān in the severest sense and makes clear to us the harmful consequences of following him. Throughout the Quran, He reminds us continuously of the fact that Shaytān is our enemy.

Allah Almighty mentions that many have lost this battle. Fending off the whispers of Shaytān and guarding against his plots is a difficult task indeed.

وَلَقَدْ أَضَلَّ مِنكُمْ جِبِلًّا كَثِيرًا ۖ أَفَلَمْ تَكُونُوا۟ تَعْقِلُونَ ﴿٦٢﴾

"But he did lead astray a great multitude of you.
Did you not, then, understand?"
(Sūrah Yā-Sīn, 36:62)

As Ustadha Yasmeen explains:

Shaytān attacks us indifferent ways depending on our state.

→ When we are at a spiritual high, he comes at us through arrogance and self-righteousness. He tries to make us pleased with our deeds, to make us believe we are perfect, superior, that it is others who need to change. We start to go on a harām police rampage. Although offering sincere advice is a crucial part of our faith, our sincerity is tainted when we begin to shift the focus from fixing ourselves to fixing everyone else (as we think we are already perfect).

→ For those who have knowledge, Shaytān will try to make them feel proud and self-reliant.

→ When we are at a spiritual low, Shaytān comes at us through despair. He tries to make us believe that we are so far and so low, that we should just give up.

→ When we commit a sin, he convinces us that there's no point in praying or going to the masjid because we would be like 'hypocrites' if we did.

→ He makes us believe that 'religious people' are all judgemental, so it's better to stick with our present company, as they don't judge us.

→ When we fail to be a 'perfect Muslim', he convinces us that we might as well give up whatever obedience we are committed to. For instance, if we are of those wearing hijāb (outer garment covering from head to toe), Shaytān may whisper to take off our hijāb, saying, "Hijāb is only for perfect people." He would make us forget or brush off the fact that wearing the hijāb is a command of our Lord. He tells us to give up the fight, because we are too far away or too low to come back to Allah.

Feelings of pride and despair are both Shaytān's tactics of deception. He uses pride to attack us in our spiritually high state and despair in our spiritually low state. Whereas no one is perfect. We all have flaws and weaknesses, and every soul is equally worthy of coming back to Allah in repentance.

To those who feel high in their spirituality, remember that no amount of knowledge or worship will make us perfect. One can always improve, and any amount of piety that we may have is simply a gift from Allah. A gift can be taken away, just as it was given. To be arrogant over the gift of piety or knowledge is one of the most dangerous and destructive forms of ingratitude.

To those who feel low in their spirituality, remember that no amount of sin is too great to repent from. The mercy of Allah is infinite compared to all the sins of humanity put together. Just one sincere tawbah is enough to wipe off all the sins we have committed.

1.2 Dealing with the plots of Shaytān

1.2.1 Being conscious of Shaytān's traps

إِنَّ ٱلشَّيْطَٰنَ لَكُمْ عَدُوٌّ فَٱتَّخِذُوهُ عَدُوًّا ۚ ٦

"Indeed, Shaytān is an enemy to you; so take him as an enemy." (Sūrah Fātir, 35:6)

The first step to overcoming Shaytān's whispers is to be aware of the fact that Shaytān is our enemy. Allah is commanding us to treat him as an enemy by opposing him. This realization will prevent us from being discouraged or procrastinate from doing acts of goodness and curb our inclination towards irrelevant and unimportant matters, falsehood, and sinning.

When we embark on any road to obedience, such as reciting the Quran, having patience, or doing any good deed for that matter, Shaytān will try to demoralize us, making virtuous acts appear ugly and difficult. He will coerce us into delaying the good until we abandon it altogether.

Shaytān works cunningly on our thought processes, moods, feelings, and emotions. If we pray our salāh regularly, he won't try to convince us not to pray, but he will engage us in an argument, busy us with chores, or encourage us to make a phone call. He will involve us with any sort of activity that will make us delay our salāh or spoil it. He whispers to us to stay in bed 'just five minutes more' so that we fall asleep again and miss the Fajr Prayer.

The guilt we feel when we delay or miss our salāh would, in turn, affect our mood and make us misbehave, thus taking us from one sin to another. This is the wicked manner in which Shaytān works.

1.2.2 Refuting the whispers of Shaytān

Shaytān makes us procrastinate in carrying out our obligations and acts of piety. If we intend or begin to do something good, Shaytān says, "Don't do it." If he can't stop us, he says, "Do it later." If he can't get us to put it off, he says, "Hurry up, do it quickly." If that doesn't work, he messes with our intention. If our intention stays pure, he whispers fatalistic remarks like, "What is the use of praying, doing Istighfār, or spending in Allah's path when you are going to Hell anyway?" These are classic tricks which he uses to discourage us from doing good.

How do we refute Shaytān's whispers?

Depending on the different technique used by Shaytān and whether his whispers attempt to discourage us from doing spiritual acts (like salāh) or worldly ones (like household chores), we must respond accordingly, as explained by Br. Muhammad Faris in one of his masterclasses:

Shaytān's whisper *"Don't do it."*

Our response **Stay Focused.**

Tell Yourself

"I need to do it, otherwise I will miss out on my rewards."

"I need to spend time with my parents and family, I need to do the laundry, memorize Quran, etc."

Shaytān's whisper *"Do it later."*

Our response **Remember death.**

Tell Yourself

"I could die any time. I must live in the present, otherwise I will lose this hour that I have in my hands right now."

Shaytān's whisper *"Just do it quickly."*

Our response **Recall that Allah loves the muhsinīn—those who perform good deeds with excellence.**

Tell Yourself

"Quality matters. I need to pray my salāh with excellence."

"Hastiness is from Shaytān, so I must not perform my good deeds in a sloppy manner."

Of course, there are exceptions. In some instances, haste is compulsory, like repaying one's debt, exercising tawbah, burying the dead, helping others, and serving guests.

Shaytān's whisper	Shaytān tries to mess with our intentions, tricking us to work for our ego instead of Allah. For example, he whispers, "***Look at your accomplished self. You deserve to feel proud because it is all your doing.***"
Our response	**Attribute all good to Allah and stay humble.**

Tell Yourself

"All praise is for Allah who has blessed me with so many opportunities."

"I have not capitalized enough on the abilities and opportunities I've been gifted. I need to tap into my abilities and be productive till my last breath."

Shaytān's whisper	Shaytān tries to convince us of fatalism, making us believe that no matter what good we do, we are still going to hell.
Our response	**Remember that Allah's mercy is far above our shortcomings.**

Tell Yourself

"I need to perform to the best of my ability. My role is to worship Allah and strive towards Jannah without questioning His authority nor waiting for results. Results are in Allah's hands."

Shaytān's whisper	Shaytān makes us doubt the validity of our actions, as in the cases of Wudū, salāh, tawāf, etc. For example, during Wudū he might whisper, "***You haven't washed your hands properly. You haven't moistened your head completely,"*** and so on. These whisperings may even occur after a person has finished performing Wudū.
Our response	<u>**Pay no heed to doubts from Shaytān.**</u>

Tell Yourself

"I have done my Wudū correctly to the best of my ability. Allah is aware of that, and that is enough for me."

The Prophet (ﷺ) said, "Leave that which makes you doubt for that which does not make you doubt, for truth leads to reassurance, and lies lead to uncertainty." (Sunan at-Tirmidhī)

"For truth leads to reassurance" means: the heart is at ease with it.

By adopting these responses, we will be able to resist Shaytān's whispers and move on in our race to fulfilling acts if righteousness.

1.2.3 Isti'āda: Seeking refuge with Allah

Shaytān's only aspiration is to avert us from the Straight Path to our Rabb, so it is paramount that we treat him as an enemy and protect ourselves by obeying Allah the Almighty and seeking refuge in Him by saying:

أَعُوْذُ بِاللّٰهِ مِنَ الشَّيْطَانِ الرَّجِيمِ

"I seek refuge with Allah from Shaytān, the rejected."

The Prophet (ﷺ) said,

"Shaytān comes to one of you and says, 'Who created such and-such? Who created such-and such?' until he says, 'Who created your Lord?' So, when he reaches it [i.e., Shaytān suggests it], then let him seek refuge with Allah and desist (from such thoughts)." (Sahīh al-Bukhari, Sahīh Muslim)

Some of the Companions of the Messenger of Allah came to the Prophet (ﷺ) complaining, "We find in ourselves thoughts that are too terrible to speak of." He said, "Are you really having such thoughts?" They said, "Yes." He said, "That is a clear sign of faith." (Sahīh Muslim)

When Shaytān attacks us with whispers to such an extreme that it reaches our belief in Allah, the Prophet (ﷺ) described this as a sign that one possesses eemān. He can only steal from a place where there is treasure, and the most beloved treasure we possess is our eemān.

Shaytān is a burglar. He never robs an empty house. If he bothers us, it means we have treasures worth stealing. We should not let these whispers hamper our progress towards Allah. Rather we are advised to say āmantu billāhi wa rasūlihi (I believe in Allah and His Messenger).

In another hadīth, the Prophet (ﷺ) said, "The Shaytān may come to any one of you, and say, 'Who created such-and-such? Who created such-and-such?' until he asks, 'Who created your (Lord) Rabb?' If this happens to anyone, let him seek refuge with Allah, the Almighty, and let him stop such thoughts." (Saheeh al-Jām'i)

1.2.4 Cling to the jamā'ah (congregation)

We need to be aware of the fact that Shaytān's attack on us is strong when we are alone. This is why Islam places so much importance on congregational worship. In fact, failure to attend the masjid (especially for men) makes us a target of Shaytān, who attacks our faith when we are aloof. Just as a wolf attacks a sheep that is isolated from the flock. Consequently, he moves our hearts away from Allah and makes us passive Muslims, disconnected with the affairs and pains of our community members.

Prophet Muhammad (ﷺ) said,

"So cling to the jamā'ah, for indeed the wolf only devours a sheep that strays away from the flock." (Musnad Ahmad, Sunan Abu Dawūd)

1.2.5 Believing in Allah's promises over the promises of Shaytān

Allah is Al-Haqq, the Most Truthful in His promises. We believe in everything He tells us. We trust Him more than anyone else.

يَٰٓأَيُّهَا ٱلنَّاسُ إِنَّ وَعۡدَ ٱللَّهِ حَقّٞۖ فَلَا تَغُرَّنَّكُمُ ٱلۡحَيَوٰةُ ٱلدُّنۡيَاۖ وَلَا يَغُرَّنَّكُم بِٱللَّهِ ٱلۡغَرُورُ ٥

"O mankind! Verily, the promise of Allah is true. So let not this present life deceive you, and let not the chief deceiver [i.e., Shaytān] deceive you about Allah." (Sūrah Fatir, 35:5)

ٱلشَّيۡطَٰنُ يَعِدُكُمُ ٱلۡفَقۡرَ وَيَأۡمُرُكُم بِٱلۡفَحۡشَآءِۖ
وَٱللَّهُ يَعِدُكُم مَّغۡفِرَةٗ مِّنۡهُ وَفَضۡلٗاۗ وَٱللَّهُ وَٰسِعٌ عَلِيمٞ ٢٦٨

"Shaytān threatens you with poverty and orders you to commit fahshā (evil deeds, illegal sexual intercourse, sins, etc.) whereas Allah promises you forgiveness and bounty from Himself. And Allah is All-Encompassing, All-Knowing." (Sūrah al-Baqarah, 2:268)

Reflecting on this āyah, we can deduce the following fundamental points:

→ Shaytān threatens us with poverty if we obey Allah by earning legally, being generous, spending in charity, and staying away from gambling, debts, and interest.

→ Shaytān commands us with fahshaa'-all types of immoralities and sinful deeds-bringing shame to us in this world, affecting our health and dignity, and furthermore, earning us severe penalties in the Hereafter.

On the other hand, Allah promises us forgiveness and bounty. If we choose Allah's promise over Shaytān's, we shall be forgiven even if we fall short of fulfilling all His commands. All that is required is sincerity and a genuine attempt from our side.

The choice is ours. Whose promises and commands will we obey and follow? Those of the Most Truthful One-He who never lies-and the Most Merciful? Or those of the greatest of deceivers, one who will admit to his followers on the Day of Judgement that the promises he made to them were false and that the promises Allah made to them were indeed true?

1.3 Shaytān's tricks

1.3.1 Shaytān motivates his troops to mislead us and cause our destruction

The Prophet (ﷺ) said,

"In the morning, Iblees disperses his army and exclaims, 'Whoever misleads a Muslim I will adorn him with the crown!' They then come to him, and one among them says, 'I remained with a person (misguiding him) until he divorced his wife.' Iblīs says, 'He will

remarry soon.' Another one says, 'I remained with a person (misguiding him) until he disobeyed his parents.' Iblīs retorts, 'Soon he will be dutiful.' Another one says, 'I remained with him until he committed shirk.' Iblees says, 'You, you' (i.e., you have done well). Another one says, 'I remained with him until he committed adultery.' Iblees says, 'You, you' (i.e., you have done well). Another one says, 'I remained with him until he committed murder.' Iblīs says, 'You, you' (i.e., you have done well) and makes him wear the crown." (Sahīh Ibn Hibban)

1.3.2 'If only' opens doors to Shaytān

We all have regrets over decisions we have made in the past or over things happening in our lives today. We often find ourselves saying, "If only so-and-so happened/didn't happen," or "If only I said/didn't say such-and-such," but we as Muslims have been taught not to let Shaytān's 'if only' paralyze us from taking action and bettering our lives.

The Prophet (ﷺ) said,

"The strong believer is better and more beloved to Allah than the weak believer, although both are good. Strive for that which will benefit you, seek the help of Allah, and do not feel helpless. If anything befalls you, do not say, 'If only I had done such-and-such,' rather say, 'Qaddara Allāhu wa mā shā'a fa'al (Allah has decreed and whatever he wills, He does).' For (saying) 'if' opens (the door) to the deeds of Shaytān."

What if things don't work out? What if I waste all of my time and effort? What if I just end up disappointing myself and others around me? These are questions that Shaytān infuses into our thought process to demotivate and divert us from doing what will be beneficial for ourselves in this world and the Hereafter.

With regards to what has passed, accept it, and take lessons from it. Trust in Allah. The whispers of Shaytān will only make us doubt our Rabb's wisdom and prevent us from seeing the benefit that exists in His Will.

1.3.3 Shaytān rejoices in his most consequential attack: marital separation

Shaytān's biggest trophy lies in causing separation between a husband and wife. He starts off gradually by creating disharmony and misunderstandings between them. He highlights their shortcomings to each other, whispering words like "she doesn't know how to cook", "your friend's wife is so caring and organized", "your sister's husband earns so well and keeps showering her with gifts", "your neighbor's husband has such a nice dress sense", etc.

If that doesn't work, he uses their loved ones to work unknowingly against their separation. For example, he may place high expectations in the heart of a mother-in-law for her daughter in-law and may even cause her to reach a stage where she wants her daughter -in-law to be separated from her son due to her disappointment and dissatisfaction in her. Ironically, all of this happens without her even realizing that she is being a partner to Shaytān in his evil mission.

The Prophet (ﷺ) said,

"Verily, Shaytān places his throne over the water and he sends out his troops. The closest to him in rank are the greatest at causing tribulations. One of them says, 'I have done this and this.' Shaytān says, 'You have done nothing.' Another one says, 'I did not leave this man alone until I separated him from his wife.' Shaytān embraces him and he says, 'You have done well.'" (Sahīh Muslim)

Hasan al-Basri (رحمه الله) said,

"If Iblīs slept, we would have a break."

We may have enmity towards people, but people can change, whereas Shaytān will never change. He is our evident enemy set on distracting us and there is no hope in achieving a settlement with him or in him leaving us alone; he will only be satisfied by our destruction. Hence, there is no room to be heedless of such an enemy, as the battle with Shaytān is never-ending. He has taken an oath that he shall take a portion of mankind with him to Hell. He promised Allah to lead us astray, and he is determined to do just that.

The Quran makes it clear to us that Shaytān is our open enemy. His tactics involve concerning us with this world so we lose sight of our purpose in life. He works tirelessly so that we may disobey Allah and find ourselves, on the Day of Judgement, entering Hellfire with him-may Allah protect us. But he does not implement these tactics without a plan. He strategizes carefully before attacking us with his whispers.

We will discuss how he formulates those strategies in the next chapter.

Chapter 2

Footsteps of Shaytān: High Order Strategy

اللَّهُمَّ احْفَظْنِي مِنْ بَينِ يَدَيَّ، وَمِنْ خَلْفِي، وَعَنْ يَمِينِي وَعَنْ شِمَالِي وَمِنْ فَوْقِي، وَأَعُوذُ بِعَظَمَتِكَ أَن أُغْتَالَ مِنْ تَحْتِي

Oh Allah protect me from my front, from behind me, from my right and my left, and from above me, and I seek refuge in Your Magnificence from being taken unaware from beneath me. (Sunan Ibn Mājah)

Shaytān works differently with different people. He uses distinct strategies with knowledgeable people in comparison to the ignorant ones, and similarly with worshippers in comparison to the sinners.

He will never instruct a strong worshipper not to pray. Instead, he will get him caught up in certain tasks, like completing an unfinished chore or answering a missed call, and thus make him ruin his prayer or miss it without realizing that its time has passed.

Shaytān attacks the psyche of humans using his experience. Despite being warned beforehand, Adam (عليه السلام) fell into Shaytān's trap of deception due to his lack of experience with his devilish ways. He (عليه السلام) was clueless of Shaytān's methodology.

When Adam (عليه السلام) was enjoying his life in Paradise, Shaytān didn't say to him, "You are having so much fun, why don't you disobey Allah?" He knew this would not work, so he came to Adam (عليه السلام) through his weakness. He tempted him with a life of eternity in

Paradise.

فَوَسْوَسَ إِلَيْهِ ٱلشَّيْطَٰنُ قَالَ يَٰٓـَٔادَمُ هَلْ أَدُلُّكَ عَلَىٰ شَجَرَةِ ٱلْخُلْدِ وَمُلْكٍ لَّا يَبْلَىٰ ﴿١٢٠﴾

"Then Shaytān whispered to him, saying: 'O Adam! Shall I lead you to the tree of eternity and to a kingdom that will never waste away?'" (Sūrah Ta-Ha, 20:120)

If our conscience is alert, Shaytān will not explicitly instruct us to disobey Allah. He will not attack us head-on but through curves and loops. That is how he makes us disobey Allah; with actions we would never have imagined doing.

He will make the righteous Muslim commit sins which he hated in the first place. After the sin is done, Shaytān will drag him into a bigger mess by making him lose hope in himself. He will burden him with feelings of extreme grief and shame and bring him to a point where he no longer feels worthy of going back to Allah and seeking His forgiveness. Though feeling remorseful upon committing a sin is the first step to tawbah, going to extremes in one's remorse leads to developing feelings of unworthiness and prevents a Muslim from moving forward in his path to Allah. That is exactly what Shaytān is aiming to achieve.

He will let us perform seventy good deeds only to trap us in a single, greater sin which will not only erase all the good that we did but plunge us further into more sin. Which act do you think is more severe in consequence: shirk, or eating pork and committing zina? No doubt shirk is, but Shaytān makes it appear lighter in severity as compared to eating pork and committing zina. We generally show less sensitivity to the idea of someone worshipping an idol as opposed to that of someone committing zina or drinking wine, although the former case should be what upsets us more.

Shaytān's plans are never random. He does not attack us without having first studied and analyzed our situation. His strategy is four-pronged:

1. He identifies and analyzes our weaknesses.

2. He beautifies the sin he chooses to trap us with, in accordance with our weakness.

3. He shows us how to justify the sin, so that disobedience to Allah becomes insignificant to us.

4. He opens the doors of either extreme hope or despair, reminding us how forgiving Allah is so we can continue to sin and repent later, or making us despair of Allah's mercy so we end up feeling unworthy and never repent.

Using this strategy, our open enemy customizes every assault, each one synchronized to our weaknesses, whether it be lust, greed, or anger. If one method doesn't work, he tries another. Shaytān never gives up, not even at the moment of death when the person is at the peak of his weaknesses. He is steadfast and committed to his mission of leading mankind to Hell with him.

2.1 Let us analyze the footsteps of Shaytān.

2.1.1 The first footstep of Shaytān: Kufr and Shirk

2.1.1.1 Kufr

Kufr can be classified as 'major' and 'minor'.

a) Major kufr:

Major kufr refers to denying, concealing, or disbelieving in one or more of the five pillars of Islam partly or completely, namely: Allah, His angels, His Books, His Prophets, the Day of Judgement, and His Divine Decree (both, the good and the bad).

Committing major kufr takes one out of the realm of Islam until he does tawbah. A person who dies on kufr is destined to Hell.

إِنَّ ٱللَّهَ لَعَنَ ٱلْكَٰفِرِينَ وَأَعَدَّ لَهُمْ سَعِيرًا ﴿٦٤﴾

"Verily, Allah has cursed the disbelievers, and has prepared for them a flaming Fire [i.e., Hell]."
(Sūrah al-Ahzāb, 33:64)

Protection

Returning to the fold of Islam by doing tawbah and believing in all that Islam has entitled us to believe in.

b) Minor kufr:

Showing ingratitude is minor kufr. After Shaytān was cursed by Allah and expelled from Paradise, he challenged Allah and claimed that he would cause most humans to be ungrateful through his whispers. He is striving endlessly to fulfill his challenge.

ثُمَّ لَآتِيَنَّهُم مِّنۢ بَيۡنِ أَيۡدِيهِمۡ وَمِنۡ خَلۡفِهِمۡ وَعَنۡ أَيۡمَٰنِهِمۡ
وَعَن شَمَآئِلِهِمۡۖ وَلَا تَجِدُ أَكۡثَرَهُمۡ شَٰكِرِينَ ١٧

"Then I will come to them from before them and behind them, from their right and from their left, and You will not find most of them as thankful ones" (Sūrah al-Araf, 7:17)

The Messenger of Allah (ﷺ) said, *"Do you not know what your Lord said? (He said:) 'I do not send any blessing upon My slaves but a group among them become disbelievers thereby because they refer to the stars and attribute things to the stars.'"* (Sahīh al-Bukhari)

This hadīth explains that if a person attributes rainfall to the stars by believing that they caused it when in fact Allah has not made the stars a means of causing rainfall, then that is a kind of ingratitude towards the blessing of rainfall from Allah and a form of kufr. In contrast, if a person believes that the stars are controlling the universe and they are the ones that cause the rain to fall, then this is associating partners with Allah, i.e., major shirk.

Protection

In order to defeat Shaytān's ploy and prove our servitude to Allah, we need to strive to be grateful to Allah by:

→ Being mindful of Allah's blessings in our life.

→ Attributing blessings towards Allah alone (this does not imply we do not appreciate those through whom the blessings reach us. In fact, it is encouraged to say words of thanks and appreciation to those who do good to us).

→ Using these blessings for righteous and beneficial causes which are pleasing to Him.

... إِن تَكْفُرُوا فَإِنَّ ٱللَّهَ غَنِيٌّ عَنكُمْ وَلَا يَرْضَىٰ لِعِبَادِهِ
الْكُفْرَ وَإِن تَشْكُرُوا يَرْضَهُ لَكُمْ

"If you disbelieve, then verily, Allah is not in need of you; He likes not disbelief for His slaves. And if you are grateful, He is pleased therewith for you... "

(Sūrah az-Zumar, 39:7)

2.1.2 Shirk

Shirk, too, can be classified as 'major' or 'minor'.

a) Major shirk:

Major shirk is to associate partners or rivals with Allah Almighty in His Lordship, in His names and attributes, and/or in His right to be worshipped.

This is Shaytān's greatest leap towards our destruction. He knows that if a person dies on disbelief (kufr) or associating partners with Allah (shirk) he will never be forgiven and he will be destined to Hell. There is no hope of him entering Paradise.

Allah says about the punishment for someone who dies while committing major shirk:

إِنَّهُۥ مَن يُشۡرِكۡ بِٱللَّهِ فَقَدۡ حَرَّمَ ٱللَّهُ عَلَيۡهِ ٱلۡجَنَّةَ وَمَأۡوَىٰهُ ٱلنَّارُۖ ﴿٧٢﴾

"Surely, whoever associates others with Allah (in worship), Allah will make Paradise forbidden to him and his final home will be the Fire [i.e., Hell]." (Sūrah al-Mā'idah, 5:72)

To achieve his evil goals, Shaytān first lures mankind towards committing different forms of shirk and kufr, such as invoking the dead and practicing magic.

Below are some examples of shirk and how we can protect ourselves against them:

Any form of worship (salāh, du'a, offering sacrifice, etc.) that is done for other than Allah (such as prophets, saints, or gravesites) believing that they can hear us or answer our prayers. Oftentimes, when a Muslim finds that his/her problems are not solved even after making repeated du'a and after taking the means of protection that are prescribed in the Quran and Sunnah, Shaytān whispers to him that his du'a is not enough and that he needs to seek help using tangible means like t'awīdh for protection. This is, in fact, his invitation to commit shirk.

Protection
A believer does not lose hope in his du'a to Allah. He knows that if any harm befalls him, even after making du'a and seeking protection, it is a matter decreed by Allah, the Most Wise, the Most Loving. So he submits to Allah's will and continues to take the means for resolving the problem.

Seeking from others that which only Allah can give (e.g., children, wealth, forgiveness, cure, protection, Paradise, etc.).

Protection
A believer knows that the source of all sustenance is Allah Almighty. Although He chooses the means by which we receive His blessings and provisions, such as through employers,

doctors, family supporters, and so on, ultimately, He is the sole provider for all of His creations. So the believer does not depend on these means for his sustenance. Rather, he places his reliance on Allah and seeks provision from Him by making du'a and taking the necessary actions towards reaching his goals. **"And who could be more astray than those who call upon others besides Allah..."** (Sūrah al-Ahqāf , 46:5)

Fearing someone or something more than Allah, which causes one to disobey Allah out of fear of harm from them. For example, a woman abandons wearing hijāb fearing that her husband would divorce her or that she would lose her job, or a man accepts ribā fearing poverty.

Protection

Remember that the obedient slaves are more worthy of the security of Allah, the Almighty, All-Powerful.

وَكَيْفَ أَخَافُ مَا أَشْرَكْتُمْ وَلَا تَخَافُونَ أَنَّكُمْ أَشْرَكْتُم بِاللَّهِ مَا لَمْ يُنَزِّلْ بِهِ عَلَيْكُمْ سُلْطَانًا فَأَيُّ الْفَرِيقَيْنِ أَحَقُّ بِالْأَمْنِ إِن كُنتُمْ تَعْلَمُونَ

"And how should I fear those whom you associate in worship with Allah, while you fear not that you have joined in worship with Allah things for which He has not sent down to you any authority. (So) which of the two parties has more right to be in security? If you but know."

(Sūrah al-An'ām, 6:81)

Why should we fear those who command us to go against Allah's orders when they do not fear the consequences of disobeying Allah? Which of the two groups ought to feel secure - the one that is living in accordance with Allah's obedience or the one that is working towards His disobedience?

Relying on the means rather than on Allah. For instance, saying something like, “Hadn’t this doctor treated me, I would have died,” or “If not for this dog, my house wouldn’t be protected,” thus asserting that a doctor has the power to cure illness, or that a dog has the ultimate ability to protect its owner from harm.

Protection

Remember that Allah is sufficient for His slaves. There is no might nor power except with Allah, and nothing happens except by His Will. So if a person is cured, it is only because Allah chose to cure him through treatment or medicine; and if a person is protected, that is only because Allah appointed a means to protect him.

When we rely upon Allah to send us aid and assistance, His help will come to us in ways we never expected. This does not imply that we just sit around waiting for a miracle to happen. We must do our part and actively seek solutions to our problems. For example, if a person is unwell, it is not enough for him to just say, “Allah will cure me,” and do nothing after it. He must seek a doctor and follow the prescribed treatment, all the while having faith that Allah will cure him.

Seeking the means is not shirk, but asserting that they intrinsically have the power or ability to provide us benefit is where the issue lies.

فَقُلْ حَسْبِيَ اللَّهُ لَا إِلَٰهَ إِلَّا هُوَ
عَلَيْهِ تَوَكَّلْتُ وَهُوَ رَبُّ
الْعَرْشِ الْعَظِيمِ

“Say (O Muhammad), ‘Allah is sufficient for me. None has the right to be worshipped but He, in Him I put my trust and He is the Lord of the Mighty Throne.’”

(Sūrah Āli-'Imrān, 3:159)

Allah, the Most High has the utmost power which is perfect therein. His strength prevails over all of creation. If He is by our side, why then should we be fearful of His creation?

Ascribing the perfect attributes which only Allah possesses to His creation. For instance, saying that someone is as merciful, just, and kind as Allah.

Protection

Know it is not permissible to compare Allah's attributes with those of the creation.

لَيْسَ كَمِثْلِهِۦ شَىْءٌ

"There is nothing like unto Him."

(Sūrah ash-Shūrā, 42:11)

Living beings such as camels, humans, and eagles have eyes, but the strength of the eyesight that each one possesses is different. If such differences exist among created beings themselves, how much more evident would the differences between the Creator and His creation be?

Humans and animals can be merciful. However, this mercy is a quality given to us by Allah and not one that we inherently possess. Allah's mercy is perfect, whereas ours is flawed; His mercy has no limit, whereas ours is limited. Allah the Almighty is perfect and far above the limited and flawed nature of creation.

Let's ponder over what Allah Almighty tells His Prophet (ﷺ) to convey regarding this:

قُلْ إِنَّمَآ أَدْعُواْ رَبِّى وَلَآ أُشْرِكُ بِهِۦٓ أَحَدًا ﴿٢٠﴾
قُلْ إِنِّى لَآ أَمْلِكُ لَكُمْ ضَرًّا وَلَا رَشَدًا ﴿٢١﴾

"Say, (O Muhammad), 'I only invoke my Lord and do not associate with Him anyone. It is not in my power to cause you harm, or to bring you to the Right Path.'"

(Sūrah al-Jinn, 72:20-21)

Prophet Muhammad (ﷺ), the best of creation, was instructed to worship Allah alone. Despite being the Prophet of Allah, he has no power to harm, nor benefit or protect anyone. Refuge lies only with Allah. In that case, how can anyone else cause us harm or benefit?

b) Minor shirk

Unlike kufr and major shirk, committing minor shirk doesn't take us out of the fold of Islam but it is a major sin.

Being emotionally attached to some means on the grounds that they provide benefit, offer protection, or ward off the evil eye, despite such means neither being prescribed in the Sharī'ah nor proven by scientific research.

Venerating some people or things in a way that does not go so far as ascribing lordship to them, such as swearing by something other than Allah, or saying "Were it not for Allah and so-and-so" or "Whatever Allah wills and you will," etc.

Protection

Allah Almighty says:
"I am the One, One Who does not stand in need of a partner. If anyone does anything in which he associates anyone else with Me, I shall abandon him with one whom he associates with Allah Almighty."
(Sahīh Muslim)

From the hadīth, it becomes clear that Allah will renounce all deeds that are done with the intention of being seen by people or for worldly benefits.

As humans, we feel extremely upset when someone else gets credit for our work.

For instance, if someone else publicizes his/her name as the author of a book, article, or blog post that we wrote, we would get severely offended. In the case of a published book, we may even file a court case against the violator. We would condemn this act because we know that it is wrong. Why should the credits to our work be shared with someone who was never a part of it? Such are the feelings of mankind. In reality, we are also not truly deserving of all the credit as we were only able to reach our achievements with the tawfīq of Allah. So by that analogy, how would Allah, the Rabb, the Owner, and the Disposer of the entire universe, accept others being worshipped and given credit for everything that He has done and is continuing to do?

Du'a for protection from shirk

اللَّهُمَّ إِنِّي أَعُوذُ بِكَ أَنْ أُشْرِكَ بِكَ وَأَنَا أَعْلَمُ، وَأَسْتَغْفِرُكَ لِمَا لا أَعْلَمُ

'Oh Allah, I ask for your protection from committing shirk with you while I know, and I ask for your forgiveness for what I do not know.'

(Al-Albani said it is authentic in al-Jām'i as-Sagheer wa Ziyadah)

Seeking the help of Allah Almighty will help us eliminate all types of shirk from our deeds and intentions.

2.2 The second footstep of Shaytān: Bid'ah

If Shaytān cannot manage to trick people into committing shirk and kufr, he causes them to fall into bid'ah (innovation) which involves performing actions that have no basis in the religion. These actions are attractive and look like worship, but they have no evidence from the Quran or the Sunnah to support them. Rather, they are based on desires or hearsay.

Falling into bid'ah may mean one of two things:

(i) Introducing an act of worship which has no basis in Islam, such as touching graves and seeking help from their occupants, celebrating 'Mawlid', or performing congregational 'khatm' (completion) of the Quran for the deceased.

(ii) Performing an act of worship which does have basis in Islam but attaching a certain time or place for it, or a number of times for its repetition. i.e., when the act of worship is done systematically and repeatedly in a manner not originally prescribed in the Sharī'ah, then it is bid'ah. Consequently, if it is done only once or twice without adhering to that particular time or place for the act of worship, then it is not bid'ah.

For instance, there is nothing wrong with reciting Sūrah

al Kahf on days other than Friday if the reader wishes to do so or if it coincides with his daily recitation, and for which he will earn a tenfold reward per letter-the same reward one would receive for reading any other portion of the Quran. But this permissibility is conditioned on him not setting aside a specific day for reciting it other than Friday, which is set aside by the Sharī'ah. As such, he should not believe that reciting it on the special day he chose is better than reciting it on other days or that there is a particular virtue for reciting it on this specific day, which is like the virtue of reciting it on Friday.

Examples of bid'ah:

Shaytān whispers, "To avoid forgetting the intention for salāh, don't say the intention in your heart. Say it out loud."

→ But we must ask ourselves, did the Prophet (ﷺ) or his Companions say the intention aloud before each salāh? In fact, there is no authentic proof available for this.

Shaytān adorns the innovation of wiping our faces with our hands after making du'a.

→ But again, did the Messenger of Allah (ﷺ) or his righteous Companions do the same?

Reciting Sūrah Yā-Sīn every morning, believing it will make one's day blessed.

→ The Prophet (ﷺ) neither did this nor commanded us to do it. Rather, what he used to recite were certain adhkār (words of remembrance) in the mornings and evenings.

Reciting Sūrah al-Wāqi'ah to remove poverty.

→ Nobody was tested with hardship more than the Prophet (ﷺ) and his Companions, yet there is no authentic narration which mentions that they recited this Sūrah to remove their afflictions.

Innovative celebrations such as Mawlid, the night of Al-Isra wal-M'irāj (The night Journey & Ascension), and the 15th of Sha'abān fall under the same category of bid'ah, i.e., additions within our religion. Doing extra acts of worship that have no supporting evidence nullifies our deeds. Can we pray four units for Maghrib salāh instead of three, or fast until 'Ishā time instead of until Maghrib time, thinking we will gain extra rewards for doing more? Definitely not. Worship is not about what we like or want, it is about what Allah (ﷻ) wants and decides for us.

Think about it. Can anyone be better than the Prophet (ﷺ) in worship? If the Prophet (ﷺ) did not perform a certain act of worship, nor did his Companions, how can it be rewarding for us to do it?

Making us fall into bid'ah is more beloved to Shaytān than tempting us into committing major sins like consuming alcohol or performing adultery. The reason being, the one who practices bid'ah is deceived into thinking that his actions are a form of worship and thus, he never thinks of repenting. On the other hand, a person who sins knows that he is disobeying Allah and may turn to Him in repentance and thus stand a chance of being pardoned by the Almighty.

Blessings lie purely in following the Sunnah because it is a command from Allah to rigorously follow the Prophet (ﷺ)

وَمَآ ءَاتَىٰكُمُ ٱلرَّسُولُ فَخُذُوهُ وَمَا نَهَىٰكُمْ عَنْهُ فَٱنتَهُوا۟ ﴿٧﴾

"And whatsoever the Messenger gives you, take it, and whatsoever he forbids you, abstain (from it) (Sūrah al-Hashr, 59:7)

Bid'ah, on the other hand, is a mirage. On the Day of Judgement, when we will be in dire need of rewards for our deeds, we will find no reward because our deeds were never accepted in the first place.

قُلْ هَلْ نُنَبِّئُكُم بِٱلْأَخْسَرِينَ أَعْمَـٰلًا ﴿١٠٣﴾

ٱلَّذِينَ ضَلَّ سَعْيُهُمْ فِى ٱلْحَيَوٰةِ ٱلدُّنْيَا وَهُمْ يَحْسَبُونَ أَنَّهُمْ يُحْسِنُونَ صُنْعًا ﴿١٠٤﴾

"Say (Oh Muhammad), 'Shall we tell you the greatest losers in respect to (their) deeds? Those whose efforts have been wasted in his life while they thought they were acquiring good by their deeds!'" (Sūrah al-Kahf, 18:103-104)

Action without authentic knowledge is like travelling without a map, leading nowhere, and rendering all efforts a waste. May Allah protect us.

Protection:

For one's deeds to be accepted, two conditions need to be fulfilled:

i. Sincerity, i.e., deeds done purely for Allah's sake, seeking only His pleasure, praise, appreciation, and reward, and not that of the people.

ii. Following the way of the Prophet (ﷺ).

The Prophet (ﷺ) said:

"I urge you to fear Allah, and to listen and obey, even if (your leader) is an Abyssinian slave. After I am gone, you will see great conflict. I urge you to adhere to my Sunnah and the path of the rightly guided Caliphs, and cling stubbornly to it. And beware of newly invented matters, for every innovation is going astray." (Sunan at-Tirmidhī)

If a person remains on the Quran and the Sunnah, and successfully avoids bid'ah, Shaytān approaches him with the next method.

2.3 The third footstep of Shaytān: Major sins

If Shaytān fails at causing people to follow innovations, he calls them towards major sins.

Every sin concerning which a text of the Quran, Sunnah, or scholarly consensus states is a major sin or a grave sin; or has a severe punishment mentioned for it; or a punishment ruling decreed for it; or has been denounced in the strongest terms, is a major sin. (Qurtubi in al-Mufhim)

This also includes sins in which a curse, divine wrath, or warning of a punishment in the Hellfire is mentioned. Similarly, every sin in which the doer is warned that he will not enter Paradise; or that he will not smell the fragrance of Paradise; or it was said concerning it (i.e., the sin) that "the one who does it is not one of us" or "the one who does it is a wrongdoer" is a major sin.

The Prophet (ﷺ) said,

"(Of the) major sins are to ascribe partners to Allah, disobey parents, murder someone, and to take a false oath (intentionally)." (Sahīh al-Bukhari)

Shaytān has his own special modus operandi for making us fall into major sins. He will continuously whisper, making us fall into his trap and commit the sin. He will use false promises and appear as a well-wisher to lure us into it.

Examples of major sins:

i. Shaytān is devoted to making us commit acts of indecency, and he makes that happen by beginning with the seemingly most insignificant of things.

For instance, he will beautify even the least attractive woman in the eyes of a believer.

The Prophet (ﷺ) said,

"Verily, the gaze is a poisonous arrow from the arrow of Shaytān." (at-Tabrani, al-Hakim)

Allah has commanded both, men and women, to lower their gaze. However, there is more emphasis on the men in this regard, as their innate weakness is the womenfolk themselves.

The Prophet (ﷺ) said,

"I have not left a trial after me more harmful to men than women." (Sahīh al-Bukhari, Sahīh Muslim)

This is also one of the reasons that Allah has commanded the women to cover, alongside ordering the men to lower their gaze. Shaytān uses women as a tool to make men fall into sin, whereas Allah has given the woman dignity and has ordained the hijāb as a means of protection for her.

Furthermore, the rule of lowering the gaze applies to women as well. Donning a veil does not give them the freedom to gaze upon men through it. They have been commanded not only to cover their modesty but also to lower their gazes.

Allah says in the Quran:

وَقُل لِّلْمُؤْمِنَٰتِ يَغْضُضْنَ مِنْ أَبْصَٰرِهِنَّ وَيَحْفَظْنَ فُرُوجَهُنَّ
وَلَا يُبْدِينَ زِينَتَهُنَّ إِلَّا مَا ظَهَرَ مِنْهَا ۖ ﴿٣١﴾

"And tell the believing women that they must lower their gazes and guard their modesty; that they should not display their beauty and ornaments... "
(Sūrah an-Nūr, 24:31)

ii. Shaytān makes us fear the creation in order to discourage us from living a life of obedience and fulfilling our obligations, thereby causing us to sin.

For instance, he will whisper to a woman intending to start wearing the hijāb that her husband will leave her or seek another wife if she takes that step.

The Prophet (ﷺ) said,

"There is no obedience when it involves sin. Rather obedience is only in what is good." (Sahīh al-Bukhari)

A wife must not obey her husband if he commands her not to wear the hijāb; nor should a child obey his father if he commands him to make du'a to the dwellers of the graves, abandon the obligatory prayers, buy him cigarettes, or smoke cigarettes. These are all sinful acts. Refusing to do them will not be considered as being disobedient or disrespectful, as following through with them would be considered disobedience to Allah Himself.

Shaykh al-Islam ibn Taymiyyah (رحمه الله) said:

"The human being must obey his parents in matters that are not sinful, even if they are both wicked. It is the apparent verdict of Ahmad. This is in regard to what benefits them both and is not harmful. Even if it is difficult for him but does not harm him, it is an obligation; otherwise, it is not." (Al-FatāwaAl-Kubra)

It is obligatory upon us to obey our parents and husband in only what is permissible and good, and in that which does not involve sin.

iii. When we begin to feel guilty for committing sins, Shaytān will provide us with justifications and excuses through words and ideas, making us delay or neglect repentance.

iv. Another powerful deceit of Shaytān is to give us false hope before we sin, reminding us about the mercy of Allah, bringing to us Quranic verses and ahadīth about forgiveness. He tells us we can always repent later. But do we know if we will live long enough to do tawbah?

This is his trickery; to make sinning appear as something small and insignificant, rather than something grave and serious. False hope combined with sins is fatal. Imagine convincing someone to consume poison and not to worry, as he will "surely be saved". Shaytān is an expert in misleading us to commit major sins and not even consider repenting.

This is why we need to constantly seek refuge with Allah against him. If we do fall into a major sin, however, we must do tawbah making sure we fulfil all of its conditions: repenting, feeling regret, leaving the sin, promising never to commit that sin again, and if it involved others' rights, then repaying their rights to them.

2.4 The fourth footstep of Shaytān: Minor sins

If the believer keeps steadfast and avoids committing major sins, Shaytān will then call him to commit minor sins.

According to Ibn 'Abbas (رضي الله عنهما), a minor sin is that concerning which there is no punishment ruling in this world and no warning of punishment in the Hereafter, i.e., a specific warning such as a warning of Hellfire, divine wrath, or curse. Rather, minor sins involve any act that is evil (based on the principles of the Sharī'ah) and that which brings about spiritual, physical, mental, emotional, social, or personal harm.

A few examples of minor sins may include having bad thoughts and suspicions about others, keeping an eye on others' faults, or entering somebody's house without permission.

By no means should we undermine minor sins because, although they aren't stipulated with a specific punishment, they can still lead to committing major sins. Shaytān can easily make us fall into this trap because most of us do not take minor sins seriously.

Shaykh al-Islam ibn Taymiyyah (ﷺ) said:

"Adultery is a major sin but looking and touching a non-mahram is part of the lamam (minor sins), which may be forgiven if one avoids the major sin. But if a person persists in looking or touching, that becomes a major sin. And persisting in that may be worse than a small amount of major sin, for persisting in looking with desire, along with the connected feelings of mixing and touching, may be much worse than the evil of an isolated act of zina." (Majmoo' al Fatāwa)

2.4.1 How do minor sins turn into major sins?

⊙ Belittling minor sins

The Prophet (ﷺ)said:

"Beware of the minor sins, because the likeness of minor sins is like a people who camped in the wilderness where one man brought a stick, and another man brought a stick, and so on, until they accumulated a lot. Then they lit a fire and cooked their food. There are some insignificant sins which, once (they accumulate) and a person is questioned about them, they lead to his doom." (Musnad Ahmad)

Talking to a woman on the phone for the purpose of pleasure is immoral, but it is not a major sin. However, if a person persists in doing that and it becomes his main focus to call women and talk to them, then it becomes a major sin. Persisting in a minor sin makes it a major sin because this indicates that one is heedless of Allah or that one does not care about the prohibitions of Allah. (Liqā'āt al-Bāb alMaftūh)

When we belittle minor sins, considering them to be insignificant and justifying committing them, this becomes grave in the sight of Allah. Why? Because we are undervaluing the obedience to Allah. We must not look at how small the sin is, rather we must look to the greatness of the One we are disobeying.

It is always better to confess to a sin instead of justifying it. We all have weaknesses which trigger us to cross our boundaries, so we must be strong enough to choose the path of repentance whenever we find ourselves swerving from the right path.

⊙ Persisting in committing minor sins

Shaytān gives us false hopes and makes us feel good about our deeds. He will say, "Don't worry; as long as you are praying, you will be forgiven for your other small sins." This is a dangerous idea because those minor sins can quickly become major ones simply by the complacent attitude we adopt. We can be deceived easily by Shaytān, so we need to monitor our thoughts constantly and be mindful of the intentions behind our deeds.

Sometimes we say or do things which we instinctively know is not correct. As soon as we realize this, we should desist that action, give it up, and repent to Allah. For instance, we know that backbiting is a sin, or peeking into another person's purse or phone is awful. Instead of persisting in it, we should try our best to leave it. And in light of following up a bad deed with a good deed, we can even enforce a 'penalty' on ourselves, such as giving $50 in charity or performing two units of prayer-for each time we falter, so that not only will our bad deeds be cancelled out, but we also train ourselves to desist from engaging in the same sins again.

⊙ Ascribing perfection to ourselves

We should not ascribe perfection to ourselves by being proud of our deeds, nor should we attribute success to our efforts. To say, "I earn well because of my knowledge", "I never miss my tahajjud prayer", "I am the first to help people in need", "If I were in her place, I would never have made this blunder or said such rude words", "It is because of my du'a that she got cured," are all examples of ascribing perfection to oneself.

وَلَئِنْ أَذَقْنَٰهُ رَحْمَةً مِّنَّا مِنۢ بَعْدِ ضَرَّآءَ مَسَّتْهُ لَيَقُولَنَّ هَٰذَا لِى ﴿٥٠﴾

"And truly, if We give him a taste of mercy from Us after some adversity (severe poverty or disease, etc.) has touched him, he is sure to say, 'This is for me [i.e., due to my merit]'" (Sūrah Fussilat, 41:50)

It is with the tawfīq of Allah and the opportunities provided by Him that we are able to excel or perform any good or stay away from committing any wrong. Knowledge of this fact should make us humble. There are many who work harder or possess more skills than us, but Allah chose to grant us that particular success. It is only out of His will and mercy that we achieve anything. Pride is the quality of Shaytān which he wants to instill in us so that, we too, may suffer the same fate as him.

It is important to note that saying, "My brother advanced because of hard work," is not minor shirk if he believes that this happened by the Will of Allah. Rather, if he believes that his brother achieved success and fame because of his own genius and efforts, without acknowledging the Will of Allah, then he has committed shirk.

⊙ Sinning openly or disclosing sins

Another way in which a minor sin can become a major sin is by sinning in public, or by casually speaking about it or openly announcing it.

The Prophet (ﷺ) said,

"All the sins of my followers will be forgiven except those of the mujāhirīn (those who commit a sin openly or disclose their sins to the people). An example of such disclosure is that a person commits a sin at night and though Allah screens it from the public, he comes in the morning, and says, 'O so-and-so, I did such-and-such (evil) deed yesterday,' though he spent his night screened by his Lord (none knowing about his sin) and in the morning he removes Allah's screen from himself." (Sahīh al-Bukhari)

If we were to fall into sin, we must conceal our misdeeds

→ Firstly, because Allah, As-Sittir, is hiding our errors from others.

→ Secondly, when sins are repeatedly mentioned in public or private gatherings, the fear of committing such sins disappears from the people's hearts. Initially, it will become easy for the people to speak about it, and gradually it will no longer be difficult to commit it. This is how Shaytān spreads shamefulness and wrongdoing in the society.

If a righteous slave of Allah remains conscious and avoids even the minor sins, Shaytān comes forth with his next attack.

2.5 The fifth footstep of Shaytān: Wasting time with permissible deeds that gain neither reward nor sin

If the believer still emerges safe from Shaytān's first four traps, he seeks to keep him occupied with permissible matters, like sleeping, eating, socializing, pursuing worldly affairs, etc. These actions are halāl and lawful, but they may take up most of one's time. Spending time and effort in these will neither earn him reward nor bring punishment. He will, however, miss the rewards he would have gained if he had spent his time in performing good deeds.

For instance, a businesswoman (who has neither a pressing need to run a business nor is the sole breadwinner of the family) might end up using her whole day looking after her work. Shaytān will come to her and whisper, "It's alright, make money so that you can give sadaqah (charity) for the sake of Allah." This type of justification encourages her to do mubah (allowed acts) at a maximum level.

Following are some more examples of engaging in permissible deeds that have neither reward nor punishment:

A person may end up shopping for hours, offering salāh late. If that person is one who doesn't like going to shopping malls, Shaytān will bring forth the idea of online shopping.

If a person likes to cook, Shaytān will encourage him to feed people as this is liked by Allah, thereby spending all his day cooking, taking pictures, and sending them to people, while neglecting his Quran for the day.

A person may become occupied in propagating the dīn. Shaytān will make him spend hours posting religious texts on social media, thereby enticing him to waste his time reading irrelevant comments, counting 'likes', and aimlessly hopping from one link to another.

The Prophet (ﷺ) said:

"There is no moment in which the son of Adam doesn't remember Allah with good, except that he will regret it on the Day of Judgement." (Sunan al-Baihaqī)

Anything which occupies our mind more than it should, thereby stopping us from remembering Allah, is excessive. It makes worship feel heavy. Wasting an hour chatting on our phone tires us and makes us lazy in performing prayer. Principally, too much of the allowed actions make us lazy in our acts of worship.

To justify our excessive indulgence in a particular action, Shaytān brings references from the Quran and Sunnah, whispering, "You can indulge in it for an hour, then compensate with the same amount of worship later," but we will not be able to. Once we give in to our nafs, it will become greedy. So the best remedy is to cut off from the indulgence as soon as the realization creeps in.

ٱسْتَحْوَذَ عَلَيْهِمُ ٱلشَّيْطَٰنُ فَأَنسَىٰهُمْ ذِكْرَ ٱللَّهِ ۚ
أُو۟لَٰٓئِكَ حِزْبُ ٱلشَّيْطَٰنِ ۚ أَلَآ إِنَّ حِزْبَ ٱلشَّيْطَٰنِ هُمُ ٱلْخَٰسِرُونَ ١٩

"Shaytān has taken hold of them. So he has made them forget the remembrance of Allah. They are the party of Shaytān. Verily, it is the party of Shaytān that will be the losers!"
(Sūrah al-Mujadilāh, 58:19)

Everyone must look at themselves and recognize their weaknesses. Deeds which are lawful and allowed must still be done in moderation.

2.6 The sixth footstep of Shaytān: Engaging in deeds with less rewards

If the believing slave is still not deceived and manages his time well, Shaytān keeps him busy with less virtuous deeds instead of what is more preferable and rewarding in order for him to miss the reward of the best and most virtuous deeds.

If there are two good deeds in front of him, one which is lesser in reward than the other, Shaytān will incline him towards the one lower in reward. He, being our open enemy, aims to make us his companions in the Hellfire. If he cannot achieve that, he wants us, at least, to be at a lower level of Paradise, so he makes us prioritize the less important deeds. This is why the Companions of the Prophet (ﷺ) would frequently question which deeds were better in reward.

In Ramadan, the best worship is to recite the Quran, but people often waste time searching for the imām with the most beautiful recitation or the one with the longest du'a or tarawīh, even if the masjid they were leading salāh in was far from their homes.

Here are some more examples of this trap of Shaytān:

- The best charity is to spend on one's family, but people go in search of needy individuals outside their families and prioritize helping them.

Similarly, the needy people within our vicinity have more right to our charitable donations than those living far away from us, yet we often find people prioritizing charity to the needy in far-off places over those within their own communities.

⊙ When acquiring religious knowledge, the best knowledge is that of the 'aqīdah, Quran, and Sunnah. Knowledge of the faith comes first, but Shaytān may adorn learning Arabic grammar first. All knowledge about the dīn is good, but Shaytān will strive to make us go after the least important branch first. He may make us concentrate too much on the grammar, or fiqh, or Islamic finances rather than concentrating most on 'aqīdah.

Some of the best deeds which must be our priority are:

Prayer on its due time

Obedience to parents

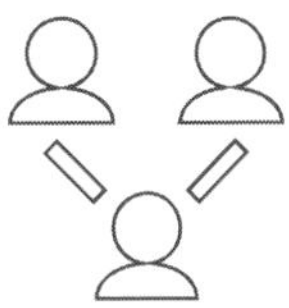

Maintaining connection with blood relatives

Negating Allah from all faults and imperfections while praising Him and declaring His magnificence

We need to prioritize good deeds according to their level of importance and continue doing them.

The Prophet (ﷺ) said,

"Do good deeds properly, sincerely, and moderately and know that your deeds will not make you enter Paradise, and that the most beloved deed to Allah is the most regular and constant even if it were little." (Sahīh al-Bukhari)

Whatever project or task we intend to start, we must begin with small steps and then stay committed. This could be for any good deed, like memorizing the Quran, praying the sunnah prayers, writing a beneficial book, losing weight, decluttering one's home or office, building a masjid, helping the orphans and the needy, or teaching new skills to children.

Start with manageable steps and do them regularly. So for example, you can memorize one verse of the Quran in a day, or spend just ten minutes on writing every day, or go for a walk two times a week for 10-15 minutes, etc. The key is to just begin with a tiny step towards the good deed, then continue doing it regularly.

Doing too much of a good deed all at once will most likely end up in inconsistency. For instance, one day we may feel extra generous and make a huge donation for a good cause but then forget about helping the needy for the rest of the year or one week we may memorize a juz' but then not memorize anything the whole year. Instead, it would be better for us to donate a modest amount and memorize a reasonable portion of the Quran on a regular basis.

2.7 The seventh footstep of Shaytān: Further harm

Shaytān, having tried everything else and failed in deviating a righteous slave, will now play his last card.

If the person still remains undefeated, Shaytān's next step is to let loose his army of Shaytān to harm the person. For example, by causing him to be persecuted or by distorting his reputation. Through this trick, Shaytān intends to discourage the person from his religious commitments. How many scholars have been tortured or killed in prison because of their commitment to Islam!

Shaytān will instigate people around a righteous person to attack him. He uses different strategies to create problems between them.

Shaytān will instigate people around a righteous person to attack him. He uses different strategies to create problems between them.

→ He will try to make those around the righteous person angry and irritated, thereby stopping him from doing good.

→ He will prompt those around the righteous person to criticize him for wasting time acquiring knowledge, saying, *"You are neglecting your home,"* i.e. Shaytān will pre-occupy the person with studying and/or doing d'awah, making him forget his obligations towards his family, thereby making them upset with him.

The messengers had their enemies too, but Allah was sufficient for them as a guide and as the One who gives victory.

وَكَذَٰلِكَ جَعَلْنَا لِكُلِّ نَبِيٍّ عَدُوًّا مِّنَ ٱلْمُجْرِمِينَ ۗ وَكَفَىٰ بِرَبِّكَ هَادِيًا وَنَصِيرًا ﴿٣١﴾

"And thus, have We made for every prophet an enemy from among the criminals. But sufficient is your Lord as a guide and a helper." (Sūrah al-Furqān, 25:31)

We too have Allah with us, so we should not be afraid. As believers, we must do our best to fulfil our obligations towards mankind, starting from our near relatives. We need to overlook their faults and make du'a for them if they fall short of their rights towards us. While conversing, we should use the best of words to prevent Shaytān from causing misunderstandings and enmity between us.

وَقُل لِّعِبَادِى يَقُولُوا۟ ٱلَّتِى هِىَ أَحْسَنُ ۚ
إِنَّ ٱلشَّيْطَٰنَ يَنزَغُ بَيْنَهُمْ ۚ إِنَّ ٱلشَّيْطَٰنَ كَانَ لِلْإِنسَٰنِ عَدُوًّا مُّبِينًا ﴿٥٣﴾

"And say to My slaves [i.e., the true believers of Islamic monotheism] that they should (only) say those words that are the best. (Because) verily Shaytān sows disagreements among them. Surely, Shaytān is to man a clear enemy." (Sūrah al-Isrā', 17:53)

If, due to Shaytān's instigation, we are faced with harsh comments and criticisms from the people around us, we should not take their comments personally nor judge their intentions wrongly. Rather, we should take a deeper look and analyze ourselves, 'Did I really hurt them for them to have reacted negatively towards me? Did I cause them inconvenience with my actions?'

If someone were to call us an 'orange', we would not take it seriously because no part of us believes that we are one. But if we were called 'selfish', it would hurt us and make us reactive, probably because there may be some truth to it. So, here we need to dig a little deeper. If we perceive that there is no truth in his statement, we should ignore it and not take it personally. But if we realize that there is some truth in it, i.e., we are selfish because we generally think of our benefits and desires rather than everyone else's, then we need to make reforms and strive towards being more generous and empathetic. We need to give preference to others over ourselves and suppress our desires whenever they conflict with public interests.

The Prophet (ﷺ) said:

"None of you will have complete faith until he desires for his brother what he desires for himself." (Sahīh al-Bukhari)

As humans we long for empathy, affection, respect, love, and generosity. That is precisely how we should treat others as well, and this will help us overcome selfishness, by the Will of Allah.

Shaytān will always remain our enemy. Even at the verge of death, he will not let us be. He will make one final attempt to ruin our chance of entering Paradise. Allah's Messenger (ﷺ) used to seek refuge in Allah from Shaytān's whispers at the time of death. He (ﷺ) would say,

"I seek refuge with You (Oh Allah) from being disturbed by Shaytān at the verge of death." (Sunan an-Nasā'ī)

After incessantly causing us so much harm, Shaytān will free himself on the Day of Judgement.

وَقَالَ ٱلشَّيْطَٰنُ لَمَّا قُضِىَ ٱلْأَمْرُ إِنَّ ٱللَّهَ وَعَدَكُمْ وَعْدَ ٱلْحَقِّ وَوَعَدتُّكُمْ
فَأَخْلَفْتُكُمْ ۖ وَمَا كَانَ لِىَ عَلَيْكُم مِّن سُلْطَٰنٍ إِلَّآ أَن دَعَوْتُكُمْ فَٱسْتَجَبْتُمْ لِى ۖ
فَلَا تَلُومُونِى وَلُومُوٓا۟ أَنفُسَكُم ۖ مَّآ أَنَا۠ بِمُصْرِخِكُمْ وَمَآ أَنتُم بِمُصْرِخِىَّ
إِنِّى كَفَرْتُ بِمَآ أَشْرَكْتُمُونِ مِن قَبْلُ ۗ إِنَّ ٱلظَّٰلِمِينَ لَهُمْ عَذَابٌ أَلِيمٌ ﴿٢٢﴾

"And Shaytān will say (to his followers) after the judgment has been passed, 'Indeed, Allah promised you a promise of truth. I too made you a promise, but I betrayed you. I had no authority over you except that I called you, and you responded to me. So do not blame me; blame yourselves. I cannot save you, nor can you save me. Indeed, I denounce your previous association of me with Allah (in loyalty). Surely the wrongdoers will suffer a painful punishment.'"
(Sūrah Ibrahīm, 14:22)

He will openly confess that he had no authority over mankind. All he did was call through tempting whispers, and the people responded to him. He did not force anyone; they came to him voluntarily.

And when his followers blame him for their ill fate, Shaytān will return the blame towards themselves, as it was their nafs and desires that led them to this painful punishment. What a worthless leadership, where the leader can neither save himself nor his followers!

Allah informs us of this spine-chilling incident that will take place on the Day of Judgement so that we take heed and use the life that we still have to return to the obedience of Allah and implement acts of righteousness.

If we want to be saved from destruction, we must believe in this warning of Allah with complete conviction.

2.8 How to remain free from Shaytān's traps?

Shaytān is waiting to ambush us from all directions - right, left, front and back. He is observing every move of ours so he doesn't miss an opportunity to entrap us.

ثُمَّ لَآتِيَنَّهُم مِّنۢ بَيۡنِ أَيۡدِيهِمۡ وَمِنۡ خَلۡفِهِمۡ وَعَنۡ أَيۡمَٰنِهِمۡ وَعَن شَمَآئِلِهِمۡۖ
وَلَا تَجِدُ أَكۡثَرَهُمۡ شَٰكِرِينَ ١٧

"Then I will come to them from before them and behind them, from their right and from their left, and You will not find most of them as thankful ones [i.e., they will not be dutiful to You]." (Sūrah al-'Araf , 7:17)

Notice how he did not say that he will come from 'above' and 'below' mankind. These two directions which Shaytān overlooked, upward and downward, when he challenged Allah to mislead us, is our fortress against his attack.

Directions which Shaytān overlooked

UPWARDS DIRECTION		DOWNWARDS DIRECTION	
	→ The mercy of Allah descends from. It is from the mercy of Allah that He has blessed us with Islam. It is from the mercy of Allah that He has blessed us with the knowledge about this enemy that we cannot even see. → Du'a ascends to Allah. › This is a 'direct line' through which direct communication takes place.		→ We place our forehead-in prostration, the closest position to Allah Almighty.

All of us commit sins, and all of us fall for the traps of Shaytān from time to time. Our Creator is well aware of this and He has revealed to us what we should do when we oppress ourselves by committing sins.

Allah describes the believers in the Quran in the following manner:

وَٱلَّذِينَ إِذَا فَعَلُواْ فَٰحِشَةً أَوۡ ظَلَمُوٓاْ أَنفُسَهُمۡ ذَكَرُواْ ٱللَّهَ فَٱسۡتَغۡفَرُواْ لِذُنُوبِهِمۡ
وَمَن يَغۡفِرُ ٱلذُّنُوبَ إِلَّا ٱللَّهُ وَلَمۡ يُصِرُّواْ عَلَىٰ مَا فَعَلُواْ وَهُمۡ يَعۡلَمُونَ ١٣٥

أُوْلَٰٓئِكَ جَزَآؤُهُم مَّغْفِرَةٌ مِّن رَّبِّهِمْ وَجَنَّٰتٌ تَجْرِى
مِن تَحْتِهَا ٱلْأَنْهَٰرُ خَٰلِدِينَ فِيهَا ۚ وَنِعْمَ أَجْرُ ٱلْعَٰمِلِينَ ﴿١٣٦﴾

"And those who, when they commit an immorality or wrong themselves (by transgression), remember Allah and seek forgiveness for their sins - and who can forgive sins except Allah? - and (who) do not persist in what they have donewhile they know. Their reward is forgiveness from their Lord and Gardens under which rivers flow, staying there forever. How excellent is the reward for those who work righteousness!" (Sūrah Aal-'Imran, 3:135-136)

Repenting after faltering and sinning is from the tradition of our father Adam (عليه السلام) whereas to persist, justify, and blame others upon committing sins, resembles the action of Iblees.

Never give up on repentance, no matter how many times you slip and sin. Allah's mercy is far greater than our sins, so we must never despair. Shaytān hates that we ask Allah for forgiveness because he knows that Allah is ever ready to pardon us.

The Prophet (ﷺ) said,

"Shaytān said,

'By Your Might and Honor my Lord, I will not cease enticing your servants so long as their souls are in their bodies.'

So the Lord said,

'By My Might and Majesty, I will not cease forgiving them so long as they seek My forgiveness.'" (Musnad Ahmad)

May Allah make us from those who always tum to Him in repentance and keep seeking His forgiveness. Aameen.

Chapter 3

Turning the Tables through Sunnah Strategies

بِسْمِ اللَّهِ الَّذِي لَا يَضُرُّ مَعَ اسْمِهِ شَيْءٌ فِي الْأَرْضِ
وَلَا فِي السَّمَاءِ وَهُوَ السَّمِيعُ الْعَلِيمُ

In the Name of Allah, with whose Name
nothing can cause harm in the earth nor
in the heavens, and He is All-Hearing,
the All-Knowing.
(Sunan Abu Dawūd)

Islam is the most valuable thing that we have as it teaches us that the only real way we can attain salvation is through submission and sincere obedience to our Lord. This is why Shaytān works so hard to derail us from it by making us disobey Allah, as he did with our parents Adam and Hawwa' (ﷺ) by tempting them towards the forbidden. Their disobedience led to their descent from Paradise. Before sending them to earth, however, Allah gave them both (ﷺ) instructions to follow His guidance and to pass it on to their progeny so as to avoid a life of hardship. Our struggle against Shaytān is imperative to our existence in this life, but as long as we follow the teachings of the Quran and the Sunnah of the final Prophet (ﷺ) we will be safeguarded from the evil that encompasses us.

The Prophet (ﷺ) said,

"Verily, Shaytān has influence over the son of Adam; and the angel has influence. As for the influence of Shaytān, he promises evil and denies the truth. As for the influence of the angel, he promises

goodness and affirms the truth. Whoever finds this goodness, let him know that it is from Allah and let him praise Allah. Whoever finds something else, let him seek refuge in Allah from the accursed Shaytān." Then he recited the verse, "Shaytān threatens you with poverty and commands evil, but Allah promises you forgiveness and favor from him. (2:268)" (Sunan at-Tirmidhī)

This hadīth gives us comfort in the realization that when a thought to do good comes to us, it is actually a guidance and a motivation to do good from Allah through His angels, so we should hasten to act upon it without thinking twice about it. Even if Shaytān places obstacles in our way or attempts to distract us, we need to ignore his whispers and take immediate action on the good thought. If, for some reason, the deed cannot be done instantly, we can at least write it down so that we don't forget about it and can address it later.

3.1 Fighting Shaytān

Fighting Shaytān and subduing him, as our scholars said, is by three means:

1. Learning his plots and methods, so he does not have the boldness to attack us.

2. Realizing the insignificance of his temptations, so that we do not feel enticed to follow him.

3. Consistently remembering Allah with our tongue and heart.

3.1.1 Learning Shaytān's plots

In the previous chapter, we discussed the seven footsteps of Shaytān and how he uses them to make us stray away from Allah.

If knowledge about Shaytān and his plots overwhelms us, we need to remember that Shaytān's only aim is to take us to Hellfire with him. Allah, He who loves us most, warns us about his plots throughout the Quran and Sunnah. Our duty is to increase our awareness of his tricks and strategies so we don't slip and fall for his temptations and false promises.

وَلَأُضِلَّنَّهُمْ وَلَأُمَنِّيَنَّهُمْ وَلَآمُرَنَّهُمْ فَلَيُبَتِّكُنَّ ءَاذَانَ ٱلْأَنْعَٰمِ وَلَآمُرَنَّهُمْ فَلَيُغَيِّرُنَّ خَلْقَ ٱللَّهِ ۚ وَمَن
يَتَّخِذِ ٱلشَّيْطَٰنَ وَلِيًّا مِّن دُونِ ٱللَّهِ فَقَدْ خَسِرَ خُسْرَانًا مُّبِينًا ﴿١١٩﴾

"(Shaytān says:) 'Verily, I will mislead them, and surely, I will arouse in them false desires; and certainly, I will order them to slit the ears of cattle, and indeed I will order them to change the nature created by Allah.' And whoever takes Shaytān as a walī (protector or helper) instead of Allah, has surely suffered a manifest loss." (Sūrah an-Nisā', 4:119)

As we increase in our understanding of the Quran, we realize the weakness of Shaytān's plans and whisperings. The Companions once complained that they experienced whispers which they disliked and would never dare to speak of. The Prophet (ﷺ) commented, *"Praise be to Allah, who has reduced his tricks to whispers." (Sunan Abu Dawūd)*

Allah affirms this in the following verse:

إِنَّ كَيْدَ الشَّيْطَانِ كَانَ ضَعِيفًا ﴿٧٦﴾

"Indeed, the plot of Shaytān has ever been weak." (Sūrah an-Nisā', 4:76)

3.1.2 Realizing the insignificance of Shaytān's temptations in the face of of Allah's promises

Shaytān can do no more than call us to misguidance and make wrongdoings appear attractive. As he has no ability to force us to do what he wants, we must strive to refute his instigations and not give into his ideas. Having strong belief in Allah's promises and trusting Him completely will render all Shaytān's attacks powerless.

إِنَّهُۥ لَيْسَ لَهُۥ سُلْطَٰنٌ عَلَى ٱلَّذِينَ ءَامَنُوا۟ وَعَلَىٰ رَبِّهِمْ يَتَوَكَّلُونَ ﴿٩٩﴾

"Verily! He (Shaytān) has no power over those who believe and put their trust only in their Lord (Allah)." (Sūrah an-Nahl, 16:99)

We must affirm and strengthen our belief that Allah is the One True God, with no partner or associate. There is no creator nor provider except Allah, no sovereign nor controller of affairs except Him. We confirm whatever news Allah has mentioned in the Quran, and we believe in all of His promises, some of which are: "Call upon me, I will answer" (40:60), "If you are grateful, I will surely increase you" (14:7), "Allah promises those who believe and do good His forgiveness and reward" (5:9), "Whatever you spend in good will be repaid to you in full" (2:272).

We trust that Allah is the One who causes any means to be effective after the right measures are taken. We believe that every chapter in our life serves a purpose, even the bad ones. We believe that the tests and trials the Almighty puts us through are never in vain.

So, whenever we feel hopeless or alone, let's take a moment and remember that He is with us, and He will never abandon us. This will prevent Shaytān from possessing any leverage that may be used to affect us negatively.

3.1.3 Consistently remembering Allah

Shaytān flees the moment we remember Allah and seek refuge in Him. Turning back to Allah is the most powerful tool we have to refute our enemy's whispers.

وَإِمَّا يَنزَغَنَّكَ مِنَ ٱلشَّيْطَٰنِ نَزْغٌ فَٱسْتَعِذْ بِٱللَّهِ ۚ إِنَّهُۥ سَمِيعٌ عَلِيمٌ ﴿٢٠٠﴾

"And if an evil whisper comes to you from Shaytān then seek refuge with Allah. Verily, He is All-Hearing, All-Knowing." (Sūrah al-'Araf , 7:200)

The Prophet (ﷺ) said,

"The devil is encircling the heart of the son of Adam. When he mentions Allah, he withdraws, but when he is neglectful, he makes evil suggestions." (Sahīh al-Bukhari)

Thus, it becomes crucial for us to constantly remember Allah by reciting the Quran, reading the morning and evening adhkār, attending study circles, and reciting ruqyah shar'iyyah, including Sūrah al-Fātihah, al-Baqarah, al-Mu'awwidhatān (the two [Sūrahs] of refuge, i.e., Sūrah al-Falaq and Sūrah an-Nās), and Āyatul-kursī.

Allah calls us "upwards" towards His path and to strive in virtue and goodness. The truest speech is the Book of Allah, and the best way is the way of Prophet Muhammad (ﷺ).

وَٱلَّذِينَ جَٰهَدُواْ فِينَا لَنَهۡدِيَنَّهُمۡ سُبُلَنَاۚ وَإِنَّ ٱللَّهَ لَمَعَ ٱلۡمُحۡسِنِينَ ٦٩

"As for those who strive hard in Us (Our Cause), We will surely guide them to Our ways. And verily, Allah is with the doers of good." (Sūrah al-'Ankabūt, 29:69)

To be on the Straight Path we need to observe the path of the Prophet (ﷺ) as he was a living representation of the teachings of the Quran. By following his example, we are undoubtedly implementing the commands of Allah mentioned to us in His Book.

When Aisha (رضي الله عنها) was asked about the character of the Messenger of Allah (ﷺ) she replied, "Have you not read the Quran? Verily, the character of the Messenger of Allah was the Quran." (Sunan Abu Dawūd)

Allah has ordered the believers to follow the footsteps of Prophet Muhammad (ﷺ). In doing so we will be rewarded with His love and forgiveness for our sins. Rest assured, in following his footsteps, we will also have guaranteed tools and strategies to combat the attacks of Shaytān.

قُلۡ إِن كُنتُمۡ تُحِبُّونَ ٱللَّهَ فَٱتَّبِعُونِي يُحۡبِبۡكُمُ ٱللَّهُ
وَيَغۡفِرۡ لَكُمۡ ذُنُوبَكُمۡۚ وَٱللَّهُ غَفُورٞ رَّحِيمٞ ٣١

Say (Oh Muhammad),"If you should love Allah, then follow me, (so) Allah will love you and forgive you your sins. And Allah is Forgiving and Merciful." (Sūrah Aal-'Imran, 3:31)

3.2 Salvation from footsteps of Shaytān through sunnah strategies

By adhering to the Sunnah of our Prophet (ﷺ) we will turn the tables over and succeed in nullifying Shaytān's attacks. Following the Sunnah in our actions and speech is the greatest means of protection against him.

The list is exhaustive, but we will mention a few Sunnah strategies we can use to tackle the footsteps of Shaytān as mentioned in the previous chapters.

3.2.1 To dispel kufr and shirk

Acquire beneficial knowledge

"Seeking knowledge is a duty upon every Muslim." (Sunan Ibn Mājah)

This hadīth teaches us that:

i. We need to prioritize learning about our religion, the Oneness of Allah Almighty, and the beliefs, sayings, and actions which cause people to commit kufr and shirk.

ii. Seeking knowledge is compulsory for every Muslim and it is the cornerstone towards combating not just kufr and shirk, but all the footsteps of Shaytān.

iii. We must also abstain from seeking knowledge that does not bring benefit to us for this world or the Hereafter, such as matters that are prohibited within the religion.

3.2.2 To dispel bid'ah

Adhere to the way of the Prophet (ﷺ) and his rightly guided successors

The Prophet (ﷺ) said:

"I urge you to adhere to:

- *My way (i.e., the Sunnah), and*
- *The way of the rightly-guided successors (al-khulafa'al-rāshidūn)*

who come after me.

Hold fast to it and bite onto it with your teeth (i.e., cling firmly to it), and beware of newly-invented matters." (Sunan Abu Dawūd)

Based on the hadīth mentioned, every person who worships Allah Almighty in a manner that He has not prescribed or in a manner that is not in accordance with the way of the Prophet (ﷺ) or his rightly guided successors, is an innovator, whether that innovated worship has to do with the Names and Attributes of Allah, or with His rulings and laws. With regards to ordinary matters, including habits and customs, these are not called bid'ah (innovation) in Islam. For example, a certain style of cooking or home decoration, using different modes of transportation, or using a new means to seek education,etc.

Shaytān appears in the form of a sincere advisor when his whispers encourage acts of worship that are actually bid'ah. We need to refute him and do the opposite of what he orders.

The Prophet (ﷺ) said,

"The best of speech is embodied in the Book of Allah, and the best of guidance is the guidance of Muhammad. And the evilest of affairs are their innovations and every innovation is misguidance." (Sahīh Muslim)

Let us consider a few daily practices of our Prophet (ﷺ) which will help us avoid falling into bid'ah practices.

Practicing day-to-day sunnahs

Category	Action
Upon waking up	The Prophet (ﷺ) said, "Shaytān ties three knots on the back of your head while you are asleep. On every knot, he says, 'The night is long, stay asleep.' → When you wake up and remember Allah, one knot is undone. → When you perform ablution, the second knot is undone. → When you pray, the third knot is undone and you will wake up energetic with a good heart. Otherwise, you will wake up lazy with a mischievous heart." (Sahīh al-Bukhari)
Blowing one's nose upon waking up from sleep	The Prophet (ﷺ) said, "Whenever any of you wakes up from sleep, let him blow his nose three times; for the Shaytān spends the night in his nostrils." (Sahīh al-Bukhari) The Prophet (ﷺ) used the term 'istinthār', which means to expel water from the nose, after 'istinshāq', which is to draw water into the nose by sniffing it up so that it reaches the nostrils and the whole interior of the nasal cavity.
Taking an afternoon nap	The Prophet (ﷺ) stated, "Take a short afternoon rest (qaylūlah) for the Shaytān do not take qaylūlah." (at-Tabarani)
When retiring to bed	When retiring to his bed every night, the Prophet (ﷺ) would hold his palms together, spit in them (a form of spitting comprising mainly of air with little spittle), recite the last three chapters of the Quran (i.e., Sūrah al-Ikhlās, al-Falaq, an-Nās) and then wipe over his entire body as much as possible with his hands, beginning with his head, face, and the front of his body. He would do this three times. (Sahīh al-Bukhari)
Regarding narrating dreams	We should not narrate our dreams except to one whom we love or to a person of knowledge who can interpret dreams.

Regarding narrating dreams (cont)...	The Prophet (ﷺ) said: "The righteous dreams are from Allah and the bad dreams are from Shaytān. So if anyone has a dream and he dislikes something from it, let him spit (lightly without expelling saliva) to his left side and seek refuge with Allah, for verily it will not harm him, and he should not narrate it to any person. If he has a good dream, then it is a glad-tiding and he should not tell anyone of it except one whom he loves." He (ﷺ) also said "He should not tell anyone what he saw in his (good) dream except a beloved person or one who knows how to interpret it." (Sunan Abī Dāwūd)
Upon entering the home and eating	The Prophet (ﷺ) said, "When a man remembers Allah as he enters his home and as he eats, Shatyan says to himself, 'You have no place to spend the night and no dinner.' When he enters his home without remembering Allah, Shaytān says, 'You have found a place to spend the night.' When he eats his meal without remembering Allah, Shaytān says, 'You have found a place to spend the night and eat dinner.'" (Sahīh Muslim)
When eating and drinking	Avoid giving and taking with the left hand. The Prophet (ﷺ) said, "...for indeed Shaytān gives with the left and he takes with the left". (Sunan Ibn Mājah)
Upon entering the toilet	Enter the toilet with the left foot and recite the following du'a: (بِسْمِ للّهِ) اللّٰهُمَّ إِنِّي أَعُوذُ بِكَ مِنَ الْخُبْثِ وَالْخَبَائِث (In the name of Allah) Oh Allah, I take refuge with you from all evil and evildoers. (Sahīh al-Bukhari)
When exiting the toilet	The Prophet (ﷺ) would exit the toilet with his right foot and say, "I seek Your forgiveness." (Sunan Abī Dāwūd)
When leaving one's house	The Prophet (ﷺ) said, "Whoever says when he leaves his house, 'In the Name of Allah, I trust in Allah for there is no power nor might but with Allah,' then it will be said to him that you have been sufficed and protected, and the devils will be far from him." (Sunan at Tirmidhī)

Whilst sneezing and yawning	The Prophet (ﷺ) said, "Verily, Allah likes sneezing and dislikes yawning. When one of you sneezes and praises Allah, it is a duty on every Muslim to say to him, 'May Allah have mercy on you.' As for yawning, it is from Shaytān. When one of you yawns, let him hold it back as much as he can. When one of you yawns, Shaytān laughs at him." (Sahīh al-Bukhari)
Disregarding doubts in prayers	The Prophet (ﷺ) said, "If one of you doubts his prayer and does not know how much he has prayed, whether three or four cycles (raka'āt), then let him put aside his doubt and act upon what he is certain of. Then, let him perform two prostrations (of forgetfulness-sujūd as-sahw) before he offers a salutation of peace. If he had mistakenly prayed five cycles, the prostrations will make his prayer even. If he had prayed precisely four cycles, it will be humiliation for Shaytān." (Sahīh Muslim)
Avoid cursing Shaytān	The Prophet (ﷺ) said, "Do not curse Shaytān, rather seek refuge in Allah from his evil." (Al-Mukhallisiyāt; Sahīh according to Al-Albani) A man said, "I was riding on a mount behind the Prophet (ﷺ) and it stumbled, so I said, 'May Shaytān perish!'" The Prophet (ﷺ) said, "Do not say, 'May Shaytān perish.' Verily, if you say that he will swell up with pride until he becomes as big as a house and he says, 'By my might!' Rather, you should say, 'Bismillah (In the Name of Allah).' Verily, if you say that he will shrink until he is as small as a fly." (Sunan Abī Dāwūd)
While sitting outside under the sun	Allah's Messenger (ﷺ) forbade that a man should sit in partial shade and sunlight. He (ﷺ) forbade that one should sit or stand between sunlight (unshaded) and shaded areas, and he said, "It is the sitting place of Shaytān." (Sunan Abī Dāwūd)
Avoid walking with one shoe	The Prophet (ﷺ) said, "Indeed, Shaytān walks in one shoe." (Sahīh al-Jām'i) He also stated, "Let not any of you walk in one sandal, rather wear both together, or take both of them off." (Sahīh al-Bukhari)

3.2.3 To dispel major sins, seek forgiveness

The Prophet (ﷺ) said,

"O people, turn to Allah in repentance. Verily, I repent to Him one hundred times in a day." (Sahīh Muslim)

The idea is not to seek forgiveness only when we have sinned, but to seek it even when we haven't. Prophet Muhammad (ﷺ), the best of mankind, would seek forgiveness from Allah multiple times every day even though he had never committed a sin.

Shaytān pushes us to believe that there is no room for forgiveness left for us, whilst in the hands of the Most Merciful, there is always place for forgiveness. Thus, we must never despair.

The Prophet (ﷺ) said,

"Whoever says subhānAllahi wa bihamdihi 100 times a day, will be forgiven all his sins even if they were as much as the foam of the sea." (Sahīh al-Bukhari)

3.2.4 To dispel minor sins

i. Follow up a bad deed with a good deed

Following up a bad deed with a good deed will cancel out the sin committed earlier.

The Prophet (ﷺ) said,

"Have taqwa (consciousness) of Allah wherever you may be, and follow up a bad deed with a good deed which will wipe it out, and behave well towards the people." (Sunan at-Tirmidhī)

One of the greatest means of expiation for minor sins is offering the five daily prayers regularly and on time.

The Prophet (ﷺ) said,

"The five prayers, Friday to Friday, and Ramadan to Ramadan will expiate the sins committed between them, as long as major sins are avoided." (Sahīh Muslim)

ii. Do not go near the forbidden matters

Anything that leads to sins should be avoided. For example, in the case of zina, Islam teaches us to not even seclude ourselves with a non-mahram from the opposite gender.

The Prophet (ﷺ) said,

"A man is not secluded alone with a woman (who is not permissible for him) except that Shaytān is the third." (Sunan at Tirmidhī)

When khalwa (seclusion with a non-mahram) is prevented, then one cannot even go near zina, let alone commit it.

3.2.5 Make optimal use of time in permissible deeds with neither reward nor sin

Make optimal use of time

The Prophet (ﷺ) said,

"The son of Adam will not be dismissed from before his Lord on the Day of Resurrection until he has been questioned about five things: his life and how he spent it; his youth and how he used it; his wealth and how he earned it and how he disposed of it; and how he acted upon what he acquired of knowledge." (Sunan at-Tirmidhī)

This hadīth highlights the sense of adding urgency to our lives and expressing thanks for our blessings, such as time, health, and wealth, by using them as opportunities to raise our ranks in the Hereafter. For instance, we should avoid going to marketplaces except when absolutely needed and avoid wasting time surfing aimlessly on the internet.

The Prophet (ﷺ) said,

"If you are able, do not be the first to enter the marketplaces and do not be the last to leave them, for verily the marketplace is the battleground of Shaytān and he plants his standard (flag) there." (Sahīh Muslim)

To make optimal use of time:

⊙ Prioritize

Start the day with tasks that matter most to you and your goals, such as performing salāh, reciting the morning adhkār, learning and reciting the Quran, etc. before moving on to the daily grind.

⊙ Plan activities around salāh time

Allah has created a framework for our daily schedule through salāh. Planning our activities around it will increase the barakah in our time and provide us with a timetable to structure our routine wisely.

⊙ Set goals

Setting goals will help us keep our focus on beneficial tasks. It will build our motivation to take the necessary actions to achieve them. While setting goals, it is important that we aim to leave behind a legacy through them, such as working towards nurturing kids to become good Muslims, writing motivational books, teaching beneficial knowledge, opening up an orphanage, or building a masjid. When a new task pops into our routine, we should go back to our goal and ask ourselves one question: "Is this task contributing to my goal or I am being distracted from it?"

3.2.6 To tackle spending time on less rewards, aim high and don't settle for mediocracy

The goals that we set in this life must be tied to our final destination, so it only makes sense to aim high! Prioritize your deeds according to what will reap the most benefits.

To mention a few:

⊙ Fulfilling the obligatory deeds first

The Prophet (ﷺ) has taught us how to excel in this life, and Allah, the Glorified and the Exalted, has guided us on how to draw near to Him. As He said, according to a hadīth qudsī:

"My servant draws not near to Me with anything more loved by Me than the religious duties I have enjoined upon him, and My servant continues to draw near to Me with supererogatory works so that I shall love him. When I love him, I am his hearing with which he hears, his seeing with which he sees, his hand with which he strikes and his foot with which he walks. Were he to ask (something) of Me, I would surely give it to him, and were he to ask Me for refuge, I would surely grant him it. I do not hesitate about anything as much as I hesitate about (seizing) the soul of My faithful servant; he hates death and I hate hurting him." (Sahīh al-Bukhari)

If we have to choose, we must prioritize our obligations over voluntary deeds. For example, we must prioritize the fard salāh over a sunnah salāh, we must choose spending on our family over giving charity to an organization, and we must prefer nurturing our children over giving d'awah to the community.

Abdullah ibn Mas'ūd (ﷺ) reported: "I said, 'O Messenger of Allah, which deeds are best?' The Messenger of Allah (ﷺ) said, 'Prayer on time.' I said, 'Then what, Oh Messenger of Allah?' He said, 'Good treatment of your parents.' I said, 'Then what, Oh Messenger of Allah?' He replied, 'That people are safe from your tongue.'" (al-Mu'jam al-Kabīr)

⊙ Performing the night prayer

The night is a time many of us tend to while away - whether it be in late night chats, attending dinner parties, watching football matches, or just scrolling through our mobile phones endlessly. But this is a time that we can use to maximize our rewards.

The Prophet (ﷺ) said,

"The best prayer after the obligatory prayer is the prayer at night." (Sahīh Muslim)

⊙ Feeding the people

The Prophet (ﷺ) said,

"The best among you are those who feed others." (Musnad

Ahmad)

This hadīth is not limited to feeding those in need. If a mother cooks and feeds her family with this intention she will be amongst the best, by the Will of Allah.

3.2.7 Building bridges where Shaytān causes rifts, emulate the mannerisms of our Prophet (ﷺ)

Allah has given us the best role model to emulate, the Prophet Muhammad (ﷺ). His worship, du'as, lifestyle, and akhlaaq are the most exemplary. If we were to follow him, how then can Shaytān get a chance to ruin our relationships?

Mannerisms of our Prophet ﷺ

Smiling, as opposed to laughing

"Your smile for your brother is charity."

(Sunan at-Tirmidhī)

"Do not laugh too much, for laughing too much deadens the heart."

(Sahīh al-Jām'i)

Beware of hastiness

Attend to affairs consciously and carefully, as the Prophet (ﷺ) stated, "Forbearance and leniency are from Allah, and haste is from Shaytān."

(Sunan at-Tirmidhī)

Avoid getting angry with family

The Prophet (ﷺ) said,

"Shaytān comes to the bed of some of you after his family has prepared it for him, and he throws a stick, a stone, or something else onto it so as to make him angry with his family. So if someone finds that, let him not become angry with his family because it is from the deeds of Shaytān."

(Adab al-Mufrad)

Giving gifts

"Exchange gifts; you will love one another."

(Sahīh al-Bukhari)

Guard against secretive speech

The Prophet (ﷺ) said,

"When you are in a gathering of three people, then two of you should not engage in a private discussion to the exclusion of the third until you are in the company of a larger number of people, otherwise that will bring him sadness."

(Sahīh al-Bukhari)

Allah, the Most High, said,

"Secretive conversation is only from Shaytān that he may grieve those who have believed, but Shaytān will not harm them at all except by the permission of Allah. And let the believer rely upon Allah."

(Sūrah al-Mujadilāh, 58:10)

It is imperative that we work towards protecting the feelings of others and avoid discord within our relationships.

3.3 Shortcut protections against our enemy

We can't fight Shaytān by ourselves. To overcome his plots and schemes, we need to call upon Allah, the Owner of all creation.

One of the Salaf (righteous predecessors) asked his student:

"What do you do when the devil whispers to you?" He replied, "I fight him back." The teacher asked, "What if he returns?" He replied, "I fight him." The teacher asked again, "What if he returns?" The student repeated again, "I fight him."

The teacher said, "This will take too long. If you pass by some sheep and the shepherd's dog barks at you to prevent you from passing, what would you do?"

He replied: "I would struggle to fight and repel him."

The teacher replied, "This would take too long. Instead, seek the assistance of the sheep's owner, he would suffice you from him." (Talbees Iblees, Ibn al-Jawzī)

With our hearts fleeing to Allah and our tongues moist with His constant remembrance we can hope to be from Allah's party, they who will be ultimately victorious.

وَمَن يَتَوَلَّ ٱللَّهَ وَرَسُولَهُۥ وَٱلَّذِينَ ءَامَنُوا۟ فَإِنَّ حِزْبَ ٱللَّهِ هُمُ ٱلْغَٰلِبُونَ ﴿٥٦﴾

"And whosoever takes Allah, His Messenger, and those who have believed, as protectors, then the party of Allah will be the victorious." (Sūrah al-Mā'idah, 5:56)

Ibn al-Qayyim (ﷺ) once explained:

"The morning and evening adhkār play the role of a shield; the thicker it is, the more likely its owner will not be affected. Rather, its strength can reach to such an extent that the arrow shot at it will bounce back to affect the one who shot it."

From amongst these adhkār, the Prophet (ﷺ) mentioned:

Whoever says a hundred times during the day:

لاَ إِلَهَ إِلاَّ اللَّهُ وَحْدَهُ لاَ شَرِيكَ لَهُ،
لَهُ الْمُلْكُ، وَلَهُ الْحَمْدُ، وَهُوَ عَلَى كُلِّ شَيْءٍ قَدِيرٌ

"Lā ilāha ilAllāhu wahdahu la sharīka lahu, lahul-mulku wa lahul-hamdu, wa huwa 'ala kulli shay'in qadīr"

"There is nothing worthy of worship except Allah alone, without any partners for Him. Unto Him is the kingdom and for Him is the praise, and He has ability over all things."

→ Will receive the reward of freeing ten slaves
→ One hundred rewards will be written for him
→ One hundred sins will be wiped away
→ He will be protected from Shaytān for that entire day.

(Sahīh al-Bukhari, Sahīh Muslim)

Whoever recites the following du'a three times in the morning will not be afflicted by any calamity before evening. And whoever recites it three times in the evening will not be afflicted by any calamity before morning.

بِسْمِ اللهِ الَّذِي لَا يَضُرُّ مَعَ اسْمِهِ شَيْءٌ فِي الْأَرْضِ
وَلَا فِي السَّمَاءِ وَهُوَ السَّمِيعُ الْعَلِيمُ

"In the Name of Allah, with whose Name nothing can cause harm in the earth nor in the heavens, and He is the All-Hearing, the All-Knowing."
(Sunan Abī Dāwūd)

Chapter 4

The Nafs and Its Reality: Self Realization

اللَّهُمَّ آتِ نَفْسِي تَقْوَاهَا
وَزَكِّهَا أَنْتَ خَيْرُ مَنْ زَكَّاهَا أَنْتَ وَلِيُّهَا وَمَوْلاَهَا

Oh Allah! Grant my soul its dutifulness (taqwa)
and purify it. You are the One to purify it.
You are its Guardian and its Lord.
(Sahīh Muslim)

The nafs is an inherent part of us - an innate portion of our fitrah (natural inclination).

The word nafs (نفس) comes from the Arabic root letters noon-faa-seen (ن ف س) which literally means 'to breathe (تنفّس)'.

Technically, nafs refers to the self or psyche. That is why 'psychology' is called 'علم النفس' (knowledge of the nafs) in Arabic.

The nafs is esteemed because Allah Almighty swears by it in the Quran:

وَنَفْسٍ وَمَا سَوَّىٰهَا

"And by the nafs and He who proportioned it."
(Sūrah ash-Shams, 91:7)

4.1 In the Quran, the term nafs is used in two ways:

4.1.1 The generic self

Firstly, nafs is used in the Quran to indicate our general self (i.e., body and soul), our individual identity.

With regards to this, the Quran describes the general self in three ways:

THE GENERIC SELF

i) The physical self

The word *'nafs'* is used to refer to the whole human self, made of body and soul. An example of this is when Allah Almighty says in the Quran:

وَاذْكُر رَّبَّكَ فِي نَفْسِكَ تَضَرُّعًا
وَخِيفَةً وَدُونَ الْجَهْرِ مِنَ
الْقَوْلِ بِالْغُدُوِّ وَالْآصَالِ وَلَا
تَكُن مِّنَ الْغَافِلِينَ

"And remember your Lord by your tongue and within yourself (in your ***nafs***), humbly and with fear without loudness in words, in the mornings and in the afternoons and be not of those who are neglectful."
- (Sūrah Al-'Araf, 7:205)

ii) Accountability of the self

The term *'nafs'* is also used to instill a sense of individual responsibility and accountability through a strong emphasis on the choices made by a person. For example, Allah says in the Quran:

يَا أَيُّهَا الَّذِينَ آمَنُوا عَلَيْكُمْ
أَنفُسَكُمْ لَا يَضُرُّكُم مَّن ضَلَّ إِذَا
اهْتَدَيْتُمْ إِلَى للَّهِ مَرْجِعُكُمْ جَمِيعًا
فَيُنَبِّئُكُم بِمَا كُنتُمْ تَعْمَلُونَ

"Oh you who believe! Take care of your ***anfus*** (own selves); no hurt can come to you from those who are in error. The return of you all is to Allah, then He will inform you about (all) that you used to do."
- (Sūrah al-Mā'idah, 5:105)

We will be under the protection of Allah when we take care of our ***nafs*** by performing righteous deeds and by staying away from the disobedience of Allah.

iii) A reminder of our human origin

Besides reminding us of our responsibility, the word *'nafs'* is also used to remind humanity of its common origins.

يَا أَيُّهَا النَّاسُ اتَّقُوا رَبَّكُمُ الَّذِي
خَلَقَكُم مِّن نَّفْسٍ وَاحِدَةٍ وَخَلَقَ
مِنْهَا زَوْجَهَا وَبَثَّ مِنْهُمَا رِجَالًا
كَثِيرًا وَنِسَاءً وَاتَّقُوا اللَّهَ الَّذِي
تَسَاءَلُونَ بِهِ وَالْأَرْحَامَ إِنَّ اللَّهَ
كَانَ عَلَيْكُمْ رَقِيبًا

"Oh mankind! Be dutiful to your Lord, who created you from a single ***nafs*** [i.e., person-Adam], and from him (Adam) He created his wife [i.e., Hawwa (Eve)], and from them both He created many men and women; and fear Allah through whom you demand your mutual (rights), and (do not cut the relations of) the wombs [i.e., kinship]. Surely, Allah is ever watchful over you." - (Sūrah an-Nisā', 4:1)

4.1.2 The specific part of self

Secondly the word 'nafs' has been used in the Quran to highlight a specific part of our self. It is something that resides within the human entity, combining all the human qualities and characteristics that have apparent effects on human behavior, i.e., our desires, passion, lust, and other emotions like anger, sadness, jealousy, joy etc.

Our nafs in its true nature will direct us towards honesty, helping others, showing kindness to parents, helping humanity, and worshipping Allah alone. While any form of corruption of this nafs, as a result of our desires, can lead us towards cheating, arrogance, immorality, engaging in mindless chatter, watching lewd scenes, and abandoning worship.

With regards to this, the Quran classifies this specific part of the nafs as being of three different types:

THE SPECIFIC PART OF SELF

i) Nafs al-AmmārahBissu' (The Commanding Self):

This is the self that brings punishment upon itself. By its very nature, it directs its owner towards every wrong action. No one can get rid of its evil without the help of Allah. Allah refers to this 'self' in the story of the wife of al-'Azīz (Zulaikha) and Prophet Yūsuf (عليه السلام):

إِنَّ ٱلنَّفْسَ لَأَمَّارَةٌۢ بِٱلسُّوٓءِ

"The (human) self is certainly prone to evil..."
(Sūrah Yūsuf, 12:53)

Evil lies hidden within our ***nafs*** and it is this that leads it to do wrong. If Allah were to leave us alone with our ***nafs***, we would be destroyed between its evil and the evil that it craves. But if Allah grants us success and help, then we will survive.
We seek refuge in Allah Almighty from both the evil in ourselves and from the evil of our actions.

Allah says:

وَلَوْلَا فَضْلُ ٱللَّهِ عَلَيْكُمْ وَرَحْمَتُهُۥ مَا زَكَىٰ مِنكُم مِّنْ أَحَدٍ أَبَدًا وَلَـٰكِنَّ ٱللَّهَ يُزَكِّى مَن يَشَآءُ ۗ وَٱللَّهُ سَمِيعٌ عَلِيمٌ

"And had it not been for the grace of Allah and His mercy on you, none of you would ever have been pure. But Allah purifies whomever He wishes, and Allah is All-Hearing, All-Knowing." (Sūrah an-Nūr, 24:21)

ii) Nafs al-Lawwāmah (The Reproaching Self):

This ***nafs*** is conscious of its own imperfections. It is continuously blaming itself and saying things like, "Did I want this? Why did I do that? Was this better than that?" This 'self' makes us take account of our actions. Allah refers to this kind of ***nafs*** when saying:

وَلَا أُقْسِمُ بِالنَّفْسِ اللَّوَّامَةِ

"And I swear by the self-reproaching soul."
(Sūrah al-Qiyāmah, 75:2)

iii) Nafs al-Mutma'innah (The Tranquil Self):

Ibn Abbas (رضي الله عنهم) said, **"It is the tranquil and believing soul."** Al-Qatādah (رحمة الله عليه) said, "It is the soul of the believer, made calm by what Allah has promised. Its owner is at rest and content with his knowledge of Allah's Names and Attributes... So he submits to the Will of Allah and surrenders to Him contentedly, never dissatisfied nor complaining, and with his faith never wavering. He does not rejoice at his gains, nor do his afflictions make him despair, for he knows that they were decreed long before they happened to him, even before he was created..."
(Jām'i al-Bayān fī Tafsīr al-Qurān, at-Tabari)

Allah refers to this ***nafs*** when saying:

يَا أَيَّتُهَا النَّفْسُ الْمُطْمَئِنَّةُ

"Oh self, in complete rest and satisfaction!"
(Sūrah al-Fajr, 89:27)

When our emotional needs are poorly met, the nafs al-Ammārah begins to take control of our feelings, thoughts, and behaviors. When it is in control, our thoughts become distorted, leading us to take things personally, to see everything in a negative light, and to believe that things can't be changed for the better.

On the other side, when our conscience, the nafs al-Lawwāmah is active, we become aware that something is wrong in the way we are feeling and behaving. We can then learn to challenge our negative thinking, leading our nafs to reach the stage of Mutma'innah. Mindfulness is a tool we can use to become more aware of ourselves, our thoughts, and our feelings, and behave in a way which is conscious of ourselves and others, despite our nafs and its lowly desires.

However, when the nafs al-Lawwāmah overpowers and overshadows the nafs al-Mutma'innah, we feel low and become distant from Allah. It is with the right balance of power that we can push our nafs towards the stage of Mutma'innah, which has the potential to connect us strongly with Allah through worship, obedience, and fulfilling our purpose of creation.

Allah has placed the recognition of good and bad within the nafs at the time of its creation. It does not require any formal training in order to differentiate between right and wrong. Whoever purifies his nafs will succeed, and whoever corrupts it is bound to fail.

وَنَفْسٍ وَمَا سَوَّىٰهَا ۝٧ فَأَلْهَمَهَا فُجُورَهَا وَتَقْوَىٰهَا ۝٨
قَدْ أَفْلَحَ مَن زَكَّىٰهَا ۝٩ وَقَدْ خَابَ مَن دَسَّىٰهَا ۝١٠

"And by the nafs, and Him who perfected it in proportion.
Indeed, he succeeds who purifies his own nafs.
And indeed, he fails who corrupts his own nafs."
(Sūrah as-Shams 91:7-10)

The Quran provides guidance to learn and practice techniques that would weaken the influence of the nafs al-Ammārah over ourselves, beginning with turning to Allah in the form of obedience in worship and repentance for sins.

Our nafs is strengthened by performing all that Allah has ordered and by doing righteous deeds, and it is weakened by disobeying what Allah has ordered and by performing evil deeds. Yet, even if we were to slip up and commit a sin, once we realize and repent for our mistake, our nafs begins to purify itself and evolves from being nafs al-Ammārah to becoming nafs al-Lawwāmah.

"It is necessary for the repentant one that he engages in worship and preoccupation with action for the Hereafter. The nafs is energetic and active; if you do not preoccupy it with the truth, it will preoccupy you with falsehood." (al-Bidāyah wan-Nihāyah)

4.2 The tazkiyah principle

The evolution of the nafs from one of 'commanding' (Ammārah) to 'tranquil' (Mutma'innah) is called 'tazkiyah' (purification). One should first determine one's own weaknesses to determine where the inclination for sins begin.

There are things we partake in without considering their impact on our nafs. For example, eating late dinners, especially at gatherings, is not uncommon today. But contemplate on how difficult it becomes to wake up for Fajr the next morning. Similarly, we forward stories about people on social media without verifying the authenticity of the news; we violate rules of the community, e.g., traffic laws, with no hesitation; and we seek means to make money without thinking twice about hurting anyone in the process or taking away the rights of others.

In Sūrah Sād, Allah tells Dawūd (عليه السلام) not to follow his desires as it will lead him astray.

يَٰدَاوُۥدُ إِنَّا جَعَلْنَٰكَ خَلِيفَةً فِى ٱلْأَرْضِ فَٱحْكُم بَيْنَ ٱلنَّاسِ بِٱلْحَقِّ
وَلَا تَتَّبِعِ ٱلْهَوَىٰ فَيُضِلَّكَ عَن سَبِيلِ ٱللَّهِ ۚ إِنَّ ٱلَّذِينَ يَضِلُّونَ عَن سَبِيلِ ٱللَّهِ
لَهُمْ عَذَابٌ شَدِيدٌۢ بِمَا نَسُوا۟ يَوْمَ ٱلْحِسَابِ ﴿٢٦﴾

"Dawūd! Verily, We have placed you as a successor on earth, so judge between men in truth (and justice) and follow not your desire for it will mislead you from the path of Allah.

Verily, those who wander astray from the path of Allah shall have a severe torment because they forgot the Day of Reckoning."
(Sūrah Sād, 38:26)

The temptations of the nafs are attractive as they offer instant gratification despite being harmful. Its temptations include all kinds of things which Allah has forbidden, such as alcohol, zina, looking at non-mahram men/women, backbiting, etc. While the permissible desires (such as eating, sleeping, socializing) do not fall under this category, it is frowned upon to be excessive in them. Over indulging in them will prevent us from fulfilling our aspirations, as it will hinder us from leaving what is wrong and thereby, lead us astray.

Just as children prefer candy to broccoli, the nafs loves what is harmful and hates what is beneficial for it. It dislikes confronting a difficult decree (even though Allah knows it to be beneficial for it) and wishes for an easy decree (without realizing that it may be harmful for it). So when Allah does not grant what it wishes, the nafs goes into despair.

4.2.1 Does that mean we should not have desires?

Definitely not.

It is important to understand that there is nothing wrong with wanting comforts and pleasures, and that it is not harām (impermissible) to love wealth and prosperity. In fact, it is a natural inclination to want those things. That is how we have been created.

Allah, the Most High, created us with the desire for wealth, beauty, recognition, intimacy, and family relations. These desires for materialistic gains are ingrained in us as a test and as a requirement to live in this world. It is not a feeling that we can just get rid of. However, Allah guides us through the Quran and the Sunnah with ways to manage and fulfil these longings in a halāl manner, one that is pleasing to Allah, and one that will help us in this life and the Hereafter.

زُيِّنَ لِلنَّاسِ حُبُّ ٱلشَّهَوَٰتِ مِنَ ٱلنِّسَآءِ وَٱلْبَنِينَ وَٱلْقَنَٰطِيرِ ٱلْمُقَنطَرَةِ

مِنَ ٱلذَّهَبِ وَٱلْفِضَّةِ وَٱلْخَيْلِ ٱلْمُسَوَّمَةِ وَٱلْأَنْعَٰمِ وَٱلْحَرْثِ ۗ
ذَٰلِكَ مَتَٰعُ ٱلْحَيَوٰةِ ٱلدُّنْيَا ۖ وَٱللَّهُ عِندَهُۥ حُسْنُ ٱلْمَـَٔابِ ﴿١٤﴾

"Beautified for men is the love of things they covet; women, children, much of gold and silver, branded beautiful horses, cattle, and well-tilled land. This is the pleasure of the present world's life; but Allah has with Him the excellent return [i.e., Paradise]." (Sūrah Aal-'Imran, 3:14)

These are the things we are attracted to in life. In Islam, our money, car, house, and clothing are all considered wealth. We adorn ourselves with these things to live a comfortable life. Allah is the One who created life this way.

If we had no desire for wealth, nobody would work hard to earn more, and no man would want to marry because it is not easy to accept responsibility for a wife or offspring.

Our children are an adornment. They beautify our lives by bringing joy, fun, love, and laughter into our lives. The route to increasing our offspring is, of course, the fulfilment of sexual desires. Allah instilled sexual desires in us so that we may have children and the human race would continue generation after generation. Without this desire, we would become extinct.

The world and anything in it can become an object of desire. That is not necessarily a bad thing unless we seek impermissible ways of achieving them or pursue that which has been clearly mentioned as forbidden in the Sharī'ah.

4.2.2 If we are allowed to have desires, then what is the problem?

The issue arises when we become consumed by worldly life. If not maintained with a balance, these desires will eventually have the ability to control us and leave a negative effect on us. They will take a hold on our heart and drag us into the depths of this worldly life where we lose sight of why we were created.

Take socializing, for example. We, as humans, need to socialize. But the problem lies in excessive socializing, wherein we may forego our prime responsibilities (such as prayer on time) and end up spending hours gossiping and making accusations against people whom we know very little about. Similarly, with excessive sleeping, eating and other permissible desires, we must draw a line in accordance with Allah's guidance so that they do not negatively impact our soul.

The key is to control these desires and to resist excessiveness. In other words, resist greed. For instance, in terms of the wealth that Allah Almighty has blessed us with, we need to withstand the urge to spend all of it on ourselves. Rather, we should include a share in it for our loved ones, the needy, and for Allah's cause. This is how we maintain a balance, curb our greed, and ultimately attain a tranquil self.

Allah, the Most High, tells us :

وَمَن يُوقَ شُحَّ نَفْسِهِۦ فَأُو۟لَـٰٓئِكَ هُمُ ٱلْمُفْلِحُونَ ۝٩

"And whoever is saved from the greed of their own souls, then indeed they are the successful ones." (Sūrah al-Hashr, 59:9)

That is why we need to need to restrain our greed-to be from the successful ones. We need to control our nafs before it controls us. We need to strive against its weaknesses before those weaknesses gain power over us.

Our Nafs has the potiential to drive us towards the 'good' path in life, filled with all that is blessed or the 'corrupt' path in life, filled with lowly desires that constantly direct us towards evil.

To ensure that the tranquil self remains dominant within us, we must strive against our shortcomings and defeat the plots of our nafs that cause us to sin.

Chapter 5

Overcoming Human Weakness

اللَّهُمَّ مُصَرِّفَ الْقُلُوبِ صَرِّفْ قُلُوبَنَا عَلَى طَاعَتِكَ

Oh Allah, the Turner of the hearts,
turn our hearts to Your obedience.
(Sahīh Muslim)

Allah says in the Quran:

يُرِيدُ ٱللَّهُ أَن يُخَفِّفَ عَنكُمْ ۚ وَخُلِقَ ٱلْإِنسَـٰنُ ضَعِيفًا ﴿٢٨﴾

"Allah wishes to lighten (the burden) for you, and man was created weak."
(Sūrah an-Nisā', 4:28)

This verse is a great proof that man is weak and vulnerable. No matter how strong he appears, or the heights of success he has achieved, or the amount of land he has conquered, a small virus can leave him helpless, a tiny temptation can derail him from his purpose, and even a meek person may rob him of his kingdom.

We need to accept this fact rather than profess how strong, grand, or intelligent we are.

5.1 Human weaknesses and their antidotes

Ibn al-Qayyim (رحمه الله) delineated our weakness and their antidotes in his book, 'Al-Fikr Al-Tarbawi'. In it, he explains that humans are created with enfeeblement. We are well aware of the fact that something, even as small as a word said against us, can easily trigger us to sin. Acknowledging and accepting this fact is the first step to gaining control overour nafs.

To overcome our vulnerabilities, we need to:

- Strengthen ourselves with eemān (faith)
- Rely in the might and power of Allah Almighty, and not ourselves.

لَا حَوْلَ وَلَا قُوَّةَ إِلَّا بِٱللَّهِ

- Beware of showing our weakness to the Shaytān, lest he overpowers us through that weakness.

Let us discuss a few of the human weaknesses mentioned by Ibn al-Qayyim (ﷺ) so that we can identify them within us and tackle them effectively.

5.1.1 Humankind is ungrateful

Allah Almighty has showered us with countless blessings and unlimited resources. He has subjected the whole universe and everything that is in it for us. How appreciative and thankful to Allah we should be for all the blessings He keeps showering on us! Yet, as Allah says, most of us do not show gratitude.

وَءَاتَىٰكُم مِّن كُلِّ مَا سَأَلْتُمُوهُۚ وَإِن تَعُدُّواْ نِعْمَتَ ٱللَّهِ
لَا تُحْصُوهَآۗ إِنَّ ٱلْإِنسَٰنَ لَظَلُومٌ كَفَّارٌ ٣٤

"And He gave you from all you asked of Him. And if you should count the favors of Allah, you could not enumerate them. Indeed, mankind is (generally) most unjust and ungrateful."
(Sūrah Ibrahīm, 14:34)

In Sūrah al-'Ādiyāt, Allah presents an example of war horses working tirelessly for their masters as a display of gratitude towards them. They are ready to perform their duties even at nighttime, never slowing down. As slaves of our Master, Allah, this is precisely how our attitude must be as well. Yet, despite Allah making us the most superior creation, we become ungrateful because of our great love for this world and its wealth.

How do we overcome this weakness?

Being grateful for all our blessings

Gratitude can come about only by repeatedly acknowledging it in the heart and expressing it through our words and actions by:

→ Recognizing all the blessings Allah has bestowed upon us and upon others, and praising Allah for them

→ Attributing them to Allah alone-not to ourselves or to the efforts of anyone else

→ Talking about the blessings in a humble manner

→ Using them to obey and worship the One who bestowed those blessings upon us

Imagine seeing the gift of a silk scarf which we offered to our friend being used as a mop cloth. Would that scene please us? Of course not. Then how would Allah be pleased when we don't just misuse His blessings of intellect, health, wealth, and faculties in trivial matters in life but also abuse those blessings by using them to cause harm to others?

5.1.2 Humankind is clearly rebellious in nature

Humans are created from a single drop. But when Allah Almighty strengthens and enriches mankind, he becomes argumentative, opposing, and unhappy with Allah, thinking he can say and do whatever he wants. Instead of being humble and grateful, he becomes proud and arrogant.

خَلَقَ ٱلْإِنسَٰنَ مِن نُّطْفَةٍ فَإِذَا هُوَ خَصِيمٌ مُّبِينٌ ۝٤

"He has created man from nutfah (mixed drops of male and female sexual discharge), then behold, this same (man) becomes an open opponent." (Sūrah an-Nahl, 16:4)

Instead of submitting to Allah and being humble for the blessings he has received, man questions, "Why did Allah not give me such-and-such a blessing instead?", or "Why did He give so-and-so that blessing?"

How do we overcome this weakness?

Being Humble

→ Feeling helpless before Allah Almighty.

→ Showing kindness towards His slaves so that one person does not feel superior to another or feel as though he has rights over the other.

→ Being humble in the interactions with one's wife by helping her with household chores and serving her.

→ Being compassionate towards the young and sharing humour with them.

→ Demonstrating modesty in one's manner of dressing and walking.

The Prophet (ﷺ) said,
"If the servant of one of you brings his food and he does not want to make him sit and eat with him, then let him offer him a morsel or two because he has prepared it and served it." (Sahīh al-Bukhari)

Submitting to Allah

The best way to combat arrogance is to completely submit before the might, majesty, and power of Allah, and to His divine law, doing what He commands and avoiding what He forbids.

Every time we feel like we are greater than or above someone else, we must recall that all might truly belongs to Allah alone, and we must remind ourselves of His intense anger towards those who compete with Him in His pride and majesty.

Remembering one's past

Remembering our past and how we were non existent before Allah made us grow stronger and increased us in intellect over time will help us stay grounded and humble.

5.1.3 Humankind is argumentative

Man, by his very nature, is argumentative towards those who challenge or debate with him. This is one of the characteristics of the nafs which we are commanded to suppress. This is because arguments spoil relationships and cause division between people. Things can get heated quickly, and tones can become extremely disrespectful. This is true whether it occurs in person or online, vocally or in writing.

وَلَقَدْ صَرَّفْنَا فِى هَٰذَا ٱلْقُرْءَانِ لِلنَّاسِ مِن كُلِّ مَثَلٍ ۚ وَكَانَ ٱلْإِنسَٰنُ أَكْثَرَ شَىْءٍ جَدَلًا ﴿٥٤﴾

"And We have certainly set forth in this Quran every (kind of) example for the people; but humankind is the most argumentative of all beings." (Sūrah al-Kahf, 18:54)

When we give in to our inclination for arguing, boundaries can get crossed and personal attacks, insults, curses, abusive language, and even negative supplications may be hurled back and forth. Indulging in constant argumentation could even make us go to the extent of lying to prove our point. All of this will lead to behavior that is contrary to the teachings of the Quran and Sunnah.

How do we overcome this weakness?

→ Accept the reality that we, humans, are argumentative by nature.

→ Work on our ***nafs*** by building patience within ourselves and by developing our listening skills so that we try to understand the other person's perspective and reach an amicable solution.

→ Try to immediately leave the place where the argument is taking place.

→ Follow the Sunnah of the Prophet (ﷺ).
The Prophet (ﷺ) encouraged Muslims to leave an argument even if they are upon the truth in their personal opinion.
He promised them a house in paradise as a reward for their forbearance. The Prophet (ﷺ) said,
"I guarantee a house in Jannah for one who gives up arguing, even if he is in the right; and I guarantee a home in the middle of Jannah for one who abandons lying even for the sake of fun; and I guarantee a house in the highest part of Jannah for one who has good manners." (Sunan Abī Dāwūd)
He (ﷺ) also said,
" ... He who believes in Allah and the Last Day should speak good or remain silent." (Sahīh Muslim)

→ Make du'a for steadfastness
To leave an argument and remain silent is not easy. We need to seek Allah's help and ask Him to grant us steadfastness in overcoming this weakness. The Prophet (ﷺ) taught us the following du'a in this regard:

يَا مُقَلِّبَ الْقُلُوبِ ثَبِّتْ قَلْبِي عَلَى دِينِكَ

"Oh Turner of the hearts, make my heart firm upon Your religion."
(Sahīh Muslim)

5.1.4 Humankind is stingy

Stinginess can be identified by a feeling of tightness in one's chest when giving zakāh or sadaqah. When somebody asks us for financial help, we start to recall our own expenses and needs, such as our child's education, paying the rent, or buying our dream house.

If we, as humans, had the treasures of the universe in our hands, we would still barely give others their due because of our stingy and miserly nature.

قُل لَّوْ أَنتُمْ تَمْلِكُونَ خَزَآئِنَ رَحْمَةِ رَبِّيٓ
إِذًا لَّأَمْسَكْتُمْ خَشْيَةَ ٱلْإِنفَاقِ ۚ وَكَانَ ٱلْإِنسَٰنُ قَتُورًا ﴿١٠٠﴾

"Say (to the disbelievers), 'If you possessed the treasure of the mercy of my Lord [i.e., wealth, money, provision, etc.] then you would surely hold back (from spending) for fear of spending. And man is ever miserly.'"
(Sūrah al-Isrā', 17:100)

How do we overcome this weakness?

→ Trusting in Allah's promise that giving will only increase our wealth. Allah promises that He will replace whatever we spend of our wealth and/or expertise in His cause with not just that which is similar to it, but actually, that which exceeds it. So, spending does not diminish any of our resources; rather, it increases them. Realizing this fact will help us overcome the greediness of our ***nafs***.

→ Taking swift action. When the thought of spending on a good cause comes to us, we must act immediately because the ***nafs*** and Shaytān will definitely attack us and try to convince us not to do so.

For example, a person intends to give $200 in charity, but the moment he reaches for his wallet his inner voice says, "Maybe $100 is enough." In this instance he should ignore this thought and go with his original intention, or go a step further and say to himself, "Why did I even entertain this thought? Now I am going to give more than what I had initially intended! I will give $250,or maybe even $300!"

Instead of lowering our standards, raise them higher to fight your *nafs*

When we do this, then by the barakah of our sincere action and pure intention, Allah will cure us of the wicked trait and disease of stinginess.

وَلَا يَحْسَبَنَّ ٱلَّذِينَ يَبْخَلُونَ بِمَآ ءَاتَىٰهُمُ ٱللَّهُ مِن فَضْلِهِۦ هُوَ خَيْرًا لَّهُم ۖ
بَلْ هُوَ شَرٌّ لَّهُمْ ۖ سَيُطَوَّقُونَ مَا بَخِلُوا۟ بِهِۦ يَوْمَ ٱلْقِيَـٰمَةِ ۗ وَلِلَّهِ مِيرَٰثُ ٱلسَّمَـٰوَٰتِ وَٱلْأَرْضِ ۗ
وَٱللَّهُ بِمَا تَعْمَلُونَ خَبِيرٌ ﴿١٨٠﴾

"And let not those who hoard up that which Allah has bestowed upon them of His bounty think that it is better for them. Rather, it is worse for them. That which they hoard will be on their collar on the Day of Resurrection. Allah's is the inheritance of the heavens and the earth, and Allah is All-Aware of what you do."
(Sūrah Aal-'Imran, 3:180)

5.1.5 Human kind is hasty

Humans are hasty by nature and rush to attain things instantly, whether it be when carrying out an assignment, cooking, household cleaning, or completing a school project. Due to such impatience, one may either miss out on important components of the task at hand or end up producing sub-standard results.

خُلِقَ ٱلْإِنسَٰنُ مِنْ عَجَلٍۚ سَأُوْرِيكُمْ ءَايَٰتِى فَلَا تَسْتَعْجِلُونِ ٣٧

"Man was created of haste. I will show you My signs, so do not impatiently urge Me."
(Sūrah al-Anbiyā, 21:37)

Staying calm and patient while carrying out our daily responsibilities will improve the outcome and quality of our deeds and help us avoid regrets. Calmness is a praised quality and can help us get closer to Allah Almighty.

How do we overcome this weakness?

Think before acting and making decisions, by:

→ Being conscious of our intention and reviewing it before doing any action. This could be regarding any activity like cooking, eating, and doing good deeds. Being conscious of Allah Almighty will force us to think reasonably instead of allowing us to make abrupt decisions.

→ Analyzing the pros and cons of our actions and decisions.

→ Thinking of the short-term and long-term consequences before making a decision.

→ Praying istikhārah.

→ After confirming your decision, take action in accordance with it, while trusting Allah to give the best outcome.

→ Ask Allah for patience

رَبَّنَا أَفْرِغْ عَلَيْنَا صَبْراً وَثَبِّتْ أَقْدَامَنَا

"Our Lord! Bestow on us endurance and make our foothold firm."
(Sūrah al-Baqarah, 2:250)

It must be noted here that there is a difference between rushing towards good deeds and rushing through them. Rushing towards good deeds shows the believer's eagerness in his search for opportunities to please Allah. Rushing through good deeds simply means to perform them in a hurry, which can spoil the quality of the actions. For example, one should hasten to perform salāh as soon as the time occurs, but not rush whilst praying so that he may complete it quickly. During salāh we must remain calm and mindful.

5.1.6 Humankind is unjust and ignorant

Allah Almighty created the whole universe and everything in it for a purpose. The sun, the plants, and even the bees, each have a specific purpose for their existence. Allah disclosed the purpose of our creation to the angels when He said that He was going to send us onto earth as the khalīfa (vicegerent) to the earth. (Sūrah al-Baqarah, 2:30). The word 'khalīfa' has been defined in the dictionary as 'a person exercising delegated power on behalf of a sovereign or ruler'.

إِنَّا عَرَضْنَا ٱلْأَمَانَةَ عَلَى ٱلسَّمَٰوَٰتِ وَٱلْأَرْضِ وَٱلْجِبَالِ

فَأَبَيْنَ أَن يَحْمِلْنَهَا وَأَشْفَقْنَ مِنْهَا وَحَمَلَهَا ٱلْإِنسَٰنُ ۖ إِنَّهُۥ كَانَ ظَلُومًا جَهُولًا ﴿٧٢﴾

"Indeed, we offered the trust to the heavens, the earth, and the mountains, and they declined to bear it and feared it; but man (undertook to) bear it. Indeed, he was unjust and ignorant."
(Sūrah al-Ahzāb, 33:72)

Before being sent to this world, all of mankind was presented with a trust from Allah to fulfil the responsibility of being His vicegerent on earth. Only when we truly grasp this reality will we work towards fulfilling this trust to the best of our ability, as has been prescribed by Islam.

We cannot afford to be unjust and react ignorantly when carrying out our responsibilities if we wish to be successful in both worlds.

What should we do to fulfil this trust?

Be fair and just when using the blessings Allah Almighty has given us by:
→ Using them wisely and not being wasteful, even if we have an abundance of those blessings. For example, we should not waste water during Wudū or when washing our hands.
→ Using the blessings in Allah's obedience and not His disobedience.

Be truthful towards:
→ Allah, by worshipping Him sincerely and abiding by His laws.
→ Oneself, by adhering to Allah's rules.
→ People through words and in dealings, such as fulfilling promises and in buying, selling, and in marriage so that there is no deceiving, cheating, falsifying, or concealment of information.

Leave doubtful matters: The Prophet (ﷺ) said, *"Leave that which makes you doubt for that which does not make you doubt. For truthfulness is certainty and tranquility, whilst lying is doubt and confusion."* (Sunan at Tirmidhī)

Do not be ignorant or careless of our worldly and religious responsibilities.

Firstly, our responsibility is towards Allah, our Creator, by worshipping Him alone.

وَمَا خَلَقْتُ ٱلْجِنَّ وَٱلْإِنسَ إِلَّا لِيَعْبُدُونِ ۝٥٦

"I have only created jinn and men, that they may worship (serve) Me." (Sūrah adh-Dhāriyāt, 51:56)

Remembering Allah is the main purpose of all acts of worship. It includes fulfilling what Allah has commanded and staying away from all that He has prohibited.

Secondly, our responsibility is towards our self, close relatives such as family members, then nearly relatives, then others which sequentially includes the whole of mankind.

The Prophet (ﷺ) said:

"Every one of you is a shepherd and is responsible for his flock. The leader of a people is a guardian and is responsible for his subjects. A man is the guardian of his family and he is responsible for them. A woman is the guardian of her husband's home and his children and she is responsible for them. The servant of a man is a guardian of the property of his master and he is responsible for it. No doubt, every one of you is a shepherd and is responsible for his flock." (Sahīh al-Bukhari)

Finally, we are also responsible for other creations, including birds, animals, trees, and non-living things such as nature, natural resources, etc. We are not permitted to kill or destroy any of them without a permissible cause.

The Prophet (ﷺ) said:

"A woman entered the Hellfire because of a cat that she tied down. She neither fed it nor let it free to eat the insects of the earth until it died." (Sahīh al-Bukhari)

Responsibility includes abstaining from what is harmful for others.

The Prophet (ﷺ) said:

"The best among you is the one who does not harm others with his tongue and hands. I leave behind me two things, the Quran and my Sunnah. And if you follow them, you will never go astray." (Sahīh al-Bukhari)

5.1.7 Humankind is anxious, impatient, and withholding

Human beings are quick to react. If one is touched by harm, he gives up easily and becomes restless. Whereas if he is touched with good; he becomes miserly, withholding his blessings.

Such is the undeniable nature of mankind. Any good or bad situation can trigger him to react in a negative way.

إِنَّ ٱلْإِنسَٰنَ خُلِقَ هَلُوعًا ﴿١٩﴾ إِذَا مَسَّهُ ٱلشَّرُّ جَزُوعًا ﴿٢٠﴾
وَإِذَا مَسَّهُ ٱلْخَيْرُ مَنُوعًا ﴿٢١﴾ إِلَّا ٱلْمُصَلِّينَ ﴿٢٢﴾

"Indeed, mankind was created anxious-impatient when evil touches him; and withholding (of it) when good touches him; except the observers of prayer."
(Sūrah al-Ma'ārij, 70:19-22)

As the āyah says, the exception to this type of human is a person who is connected to his rabb through establishing his salāh.

In order to become 'exceptional', we must observe and establish the prayer. In every unit of the salāh there exists a notion of exalting, magnification, humiliation, submission, and peace. When we are mindful about our salāh, we will quickly elevate our connection with Allah and have tranquility, patience, and calmness instilled within us.

5.2 Humankind is in hardship

Every person, regardless of his faith and background, goes through challenges and struggles in life. What makes it easier for a believer is his complete reliance on Allah Almighty.

لَقَدْ خَلَقْنَا ٱلْإِنسَٰنَ فِي كَبَدٍ ﴿٤﴾

"Verily, We have created man in toil."
(Sūrah al-Balad, 90:4)

The word 'kabad' mentioned in this verse indicates all types of challenges and hardships we face in life. We can overcome the adversities in our life by overcoming our inherent weaknesses. Even if the reason for our failure is genuine, we should not allow it to dominate us to the extent that it prevents us from making further progress. We need to keep reassuring ourselves that we can do it; with the help of Allah, we can overcome our weaknesses and hurdles.Then, we must take the necessary steps, however small, to move on.

Allah Almighty informs us of our reality not so that we may feel vulnerable and lose heart or stop striving and give up, but rather, He wants us to:

i) Believe and place complete trust in Him after striving to do our best.

For example, after knowing that humankind is hasty, we need to accept this as being part of our nature. This should motivate us to stay calm when doing any work that usually makes us anxious, such as cooking for a large gathering or preparing for a trip abroad, while trusting that in doing this, Allah will help us accomplish the task to the best of our ability.

ii) Enjoin the truth and patience upon one another.

When we see our children doing their homework hurriedly, we need to advise and remind them of the purpose of their education. Likewise, children can gently remind their parents if they see them in a hurry to wrap up the day's work and in the process become rude or intolerant.

5.3 Humankind is aware of himself, despite his excuses

As humans, we are well aware of our inner flaws. We must stop denying our shortcomings and be truthful to ourselves so that we can move forward and live a life of productivity and improvement.

بَلِ ٱلْإِنسَٰنُ عَلَىٰ نَفْسِهِۦ بَصِيرَةٌ ﴿١٤﴾ وَلَوْ أَلْقَىٰ مَعَاذِيرَهُۥ ﴿١٥﴾

"Man, against himself, will be a witness,
even if he presents his excuses."
(Sūrah al-Qiyāmah, 75:14-15)

We have a tendency to console ourselves with regards to our shortcomings. For example, we excuse ourselves with statements like, "I failed the exam because I had a headache from staying up all night with my child," while we consider our classmate to have failed because she didn't work diligently. Or a sister may say, "I made my sister upset because of my behavior towards her," but later consoles herself by thinking, "she is very sensitive."

Likewise, we cover up our faults with a myriad of excuses, like:

- *I didn't call my mum for days because I was busy*
- *I am perpetually late for work because of the traffic*
- *I cheat in my exams because everyone does it*
- *The glass mug broke because someone else didn't put it properly*
- *I lie to my parents because they are very strict*
- *I am overweight because of thyroid issues*

and so on...

How do we tackle this underlying problem?

By accepting the flaws

Accepting one's flaws is indeed a difficult task, but it is essential for refining one's character and excelling in good deeds. Acknowledging our faults only helps us become a better version of ourselves, and thus, hopeful we will raise in ranks near to Allah Almighty.

By being humble

This crucial step includes humbling ourselves and interpreting the situation as a message from Allah that we need to improve. This comes with the realization that we are meant to experience that particular 'failure', i.e., Allah wants us to experience it so that we learn through it and overcome from it. And this can only be done when we humble ourselves.

By working towards rectification

Knowing our reality and accepting it will bring truthfulness in us. Next time we are presented with a harsh reality of ourselves, instead of justifying it with excuses like, "she doesn't know my situation", "she is unempathetic and unreasonable", "she doesn't understand me and is misjudging me" etc., we should work towards rectifying our flaws. We should contemplate on what we are confronted with and think of how we can make the situation better. In turn, we'll be able to use such exposures to cease our wrongdoings and shift our focus towards producing good results in every situation.

5.4 Allah created humans in the best form

We can remain in the best form Allah has created us in by constantly cleaning and purifying ourselves, and this is what tazkiyah means in Arabic, originating from the meaning 'cleansing and purifying'.

Despite being weak, Allah mentions that He created us in the best form, giving us hope that we can overcome our weaknesses. The āyah below uplifts our spirits and motivates us to keep excelling in our pursuit of seeking Allah's pleasure.

لَقَدْ خَلَقْنَا ٱلْإِنسَٰنَ فِىٓ أَحْسَنِ تَقْوِيمٍ ﴿٤﴾

"Verily, We created man of the best stature (form)."
(Sūrah at-Tīn, 95:4)

Pause for a moment and contemplate on your eyes, posture, intelligence, and ability to learn and grow. Allah Almighty created us in the best form in order to receive the best revelation from Him. He gave us amazing blessings and subjected the whole universe for us. To make the most of His favors and achieve success through them, we should take care of our natural disposition by believing, doing good deeds, and enjoining each other to truth and patience.

إِنَّ ٱلْإِنسَٰنَ لَفِى خُسْرٍ ﴿٢﴾

إِلَّا ٱلَّذِينَ ءَامَنُوا۟ وَعَمِلُوا۟ ٱلصَّٰلِحَٰتِ وَتَوَاصَوْا۟ بِٱلْحَقِّ وَتَوَاصَوْا۟ بِٱلصَّبْرِ ﴿٣﴾

"Verily, man is in loss—except those who believe, do righteous good deeds, enjoin one another to the truth, and enjoin one another to patience."
(Sūrah al-'Asr, 103:2-3)

5.4.1 Constant purification

The word 'tazkiyah' in Arabic originates from the meaning 'cleansing and purifying'. Allah says,

قَدْ أَفْلَحَ مَن زَكَّىٰهَا ﴿٩﴾

"He who purifies it (his soul) will indeed be successful."
(Sūrah ash-Shams, 91:9)

Our mission in this world is to return to Allah with a sound heart, one that submits and surrenders to Allah, the Most High. Conscious of the temporary nature of our existence and believing that we are answerable to Allah are key focuses on our route to tazkiyah (self-purification).

Practical steps to achieve our tazkiyah

Faith & Knowledge
Strengthening our faith in Allah by acquiring authentic knowledge.

Quran
Reading the Quran with understanding.

Prayers & Fasting
The Prophet (ﷺ) said regarding this, "Imagine that there was a river at your doorstep and that you bathed in it five times a day. Would that leave any dirt in your body?" The Companions (رضي الله عنهم) answered, "No, not at all!" So he (ﷺ) said, "This is exactly like the prayers you perform five times a day." (Sahīh al-Bukhari)

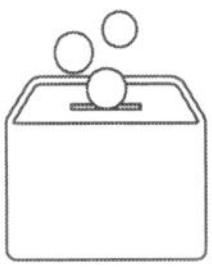

Charity
Allah says,

خُذْ مِنْ أَمْوَالِهِمْ صَدَقَةً تُطَهِّرُهُمْ وَتُزَكِّيهِم بِهَا وَصَلِّ عَلَيْهِمْ إِنَّ
صَلَاتَكَ سَكَنٌ لَّهُمْ وَاللَّهُ سَمِيعٌ عَلِيمٌ

"Take, (Oh Prophet), alms out of their wealth to cleanse them and purify them, and pray for them; your prayer will be a comfort to them. And Allah is All-Hearing, All-Knowing."
(Sūrah at-Tawbah, 9:103)

Repenting
Contemplating on our mistakes and repenting for them at the end of every day.

Self Control
Abandoning sins and forbidden acts, and restraining ourselves from negative emotions such as anger, fear of people, jealously, etc.

Kindness
Adopting a kind and compassionate attitude towards every living being on earth.

Community
Taking heed of our community and those we choose to stay around by preferring those who help purify our ***nafs*** and remain a mirror to us and a role model to follow. Failing to do so may push us to succumb to societal and peer pressures every time we are triggered by our surroundings or companions.

Through His decree, Allah not only places us in situations which bring to light our flaws so that we can overcome them, but He also guides us towards good deeds to purify us. Such virtuous deeds are vast and not limited to a few rituals. For some, their strength may lie in prayers. For others, it may be in fasting, acquiring knowledge, or practicing d'awah. And for others, it may be in sharing their radiant smile or lending a helping hand to a person in need.

So, instead of showing resistance and unwillingness to accept the decree of Allah, instead of loving to stay within our comfort zone and giving in to every whim and desire of our nafs, we need to work on engaging our nafs in constant purification.

Chapter 6

Shaytān vs the Nafs

اللَّهُمَّ إِنِّي أَسْأَلُكَ الْعَفْوَ وَالْعَافِيَةَ فِي الدُّنْيَا وَالآخِرَةِ

Oh Allah, I seek Your forgiveness and my well-being in this world and the Hereafter. (Sunan Ibn Mājah)

How often are we faced with desires from within and temptations all around us? Desires that push us to seek fun in every possible way—permissible or otherwise. They drive us to compete with our peers, just to pass the time or to maintain the status quo. We are driven to inner battles against ourselves, and we are drawn towards opposing directions in our thoughts and intentions.

→ **To do** or not to do
→ **To say** or not to say
→ **To listen** or not to listen
→ **To touch** or not to touch
→ **To look** or to lower the gaze
→ **To give in** to stress or to respond calmly to the situation

The question arises:

⊙ How do we distinguish between the whispers of our nafs and that of Shaytān?

⊙ Which one is stronger and against whom should we struggle and strive harder?

Abu Hazim (ﷺ) made a comparison between the whispers caused by the nafs and those caused by Shaytān, saying:

"Whatever your nafs hates for your nafs is from the Shaytān, so seek refuge with Allah from it. And whatever your nafs likes for your nafs is from your nafs, so forbid it." (Majmū' al-Fatāwa)

Sins start with desires. This is the root cause of all wrongdoing.

We have established that Shaytān tempts us into sinning by triggering our desires.

▸ But how did Shaytān fall into his own sin of disobedience to Allah Almighty?

It was the weakness of his nafs that led him to his destruction. Succumbing to his desires earned him the curse of Allah and rendered his many years of worship a waste.

After his banishment from Allah's mercy, Shaytān made it his lifelong mission to misguide mankind. He began his pursuit with our parents, Adam (عليه السلام) and Hawwa (عليها السلام). He tricked them into eating from the forbidden tree by prodding their nafs' desire to live in Jannah forever. Shaytān merely added fuel to the fire. The desire of Adam (عليه السلام) to live an eternal life in Paradise made him err and disobey Allah's command.

▸ The first killing on earth, that of Habil by his brother Qabil, happened because of the nafs' inclination towards jealousy. When both brothers were commanded by Allah to offer a sacrifice, and one's effort was accepted while the other's rejected due to differences in their intentions and the quality of their sacrifices, the latter developed a feeling of jealousy which led to murdering his own brother.

What does this prove to us?

6.1 Who is stronger as an enemy:the nafs or Shaytān?

Let us compare...

SHAYTAN	NAFS
Shaytān is not stubborn.	**The *nafs* is adamant and stubborn.**
Shaytān makes a sin appear attractive until we fall into it. If Shaytān is unable to achieve that, he moves on to another sin, and if that does not work, he moves on to a third, and so on.	The *nafs* urges a person to commit a specific sin and repeatedly seeks to make him do it. The *nafs* is like a stubborn child; neither does it budge until it gets what it wants, nor does it accept alternatives.
Shaytān can only incite us to do shirk and other acts of disobedience. He cannot take hold of our limbs and make us sin.	**The *nafs* forces us to listen to it, rather than allowing us to obey Allah's commands. It can take control of our mind and limbs.**
	Thus, the *nafs* does what it desires even if it goes against Allah's commands and enforces its will so that we act according to its whims and wishes. Allah speaks about this in the Quran, "Have you seen the one who takes as his god his own desire? Then would you be responsible for him?" (Sūrah al-Furqān, 25:43)

SHAYTAN	NAFS
Shaytān is an external enemy.	**The *nafs* is an in-house enemy.**
He can only succeed if the inner one (the *nafs*) cooperates with it. If the *nafs* does its tazkiyah (inner purification) and refuses to collaborate with him, his attacks will not work.	We need to fight the *nafs* first in order to save ourselves from both internal and external harm.
Shaytān's plots are weak.	**The *nafs'* plotting is strong.**
Allah mentions this in the Quran, "Indeed, the plot of Shaytān has ever been weak." (Sūrah an-Nisā', 4:76)	The *nafs* does not desist until it gets what it desires. Thereafter, it constantly presents justification for the wrong that it does. For example, the *nafs* says, "Accept interest earnings so that you can survive in this world; your job may not be lawful but you need to continue in order to feed your family."
Shaytān goes away when we remember Allah.	**There is no limit to the desires of the *nafs*. It keeps wanting more and more.**

From the above comparison, we realize that the nafs is more of a vicious enemy to us than Shaytān. Shaytān is like a fire that only lights a matchstick. Although he plants negative thoughts into our minds and evil whispers into our hearts, it is the weakness of our nafs that ultimately makes us slip and act upon those provocations, unless Allah protects us with His mercy.

6.2 Shaytān plays on our nafs

We must beware of giving Shaytān a chance to attack us through our desires. We must guard our nafs from making itself an ilāh (deity) and from becoming a force so strong that it compels us to obey its commands over the commands of Allah.

Only 3% of matters mentioned in the Quran are made forbidden for us. It is within this 3% that Shaytān adorns and beautifies evil for us, as per our likes and dislikes. His agenda is to make us slip by means of manipulating the desires of our nafs—just as he did with our father, Adam (عليه السلام).

وَقُلْنَا يَـٰٓـَٔادَمُ ٱسْكُنْ أَنتَ وَزَوْجُكَ ٱلْجَنَّةَ وَكُلَا مِنْهَا رَغَدًا حَيْثُ شِئْتُمَا

وَلَا تَقْرَبَا هَـٰذِهِ ٱلشَّجَرَةَ فَتَكُونَا مِنَ ٱلظَّـٰلِمِينَ ﴿٣٥﴾

"And We said: 'O Adam! Live with your wife in Paradise and eat as freely as you please, but do not approach this tree, or else you will be wrongdoers.'"
(Sūrah al-Baqarah, 2:35)

فَأَزَلَّهُمَا ٱلشَّيْطَـٰنُ عَنْهَا فَأَخْرَجَهُمَا مِمَّا كَانَا فِيهِ ۖ

وَقُلْنَا ٱهْبِطُوا۟ بَعْضُكُمْ لِبَعْضٍ عَدُوٌّ ۖ وَلَكُمْ فِى ٱلْأَرْضِ مُسْتَقَرٌّ وَمَتَـٰعٌ إِلَىٰ حِينٍ ﴿٣٦﴾

"Then Shaytān made them slip therefrom [i.e., Paradise], and got them out from that in which they were."
(Sūrah al-Baqarah, 2:36)

6.3 Dangerous acts

6.3.1 Making the nafsan ilāh

Raising the status of the nafs to that of an ilāh is a highly dangerous act. Yet, there are plenty of instances when we may do just that without even realizing it. Here are a few examples on how the nafs can make itself an ilāh:

Example 1

Allah commands us to place our trust in Him alone, but our *nafs* inclines towards trusting the means rather than the creator of those means. This is true in the case of blindly trusting a doctor or medicines for curing an illness, and in the case of solely believing in one's education, skills, or social media for increasing wealth.

وَعَلَى اللّٰهِ فَتَوَكَّلُوا إِن كُنتُم مُّؤْمِنِينَ

"And place your trust in Allah if you are indeed believers."
(Sūrah al-Mā'idah, 5:23)

Trusting Allah Almighty alone does not mean that we neglect taking the means to achieving what we want, whether it be for curing an illness, for increasing our wealth, or for any other matter. Rather, it includes actively seeking the means while believing that He, the All-Powerful, alone affects the outcome.

Example 2

Allah commands us to choose good words whilst speaking, but many a time we do the complete opposite. We give in to the commands of our *nafs* and use rude, harsh, and derogatory words, even towards our loved ones.

قَوْلٌ مَّعْرُوفٌ وَمَغْفِرَةٌ خَيْرٌ مِّن صَدَقَةٍ يَتْبَعُهَا أَذًى وَاللَّهُ غَنِيٌّ حَلِيمٌ

"Kind words and forgiving faults are better than sadaqah (charity) followed by injury. And Allah is Rich (free of all wants) and He is Most-Forbearing."
(Sūrah al-Baqarah, 2:263)

Example 3

Allah Almighty commands us to share from what He has provided us. But our *nafs* demands that we keep it all for ourselves, directing us to be greedy and stingy.

يَا أَيُّهَا الَّذِينَ آمَنُوا أَنفِقُوا مِمَّا رَزَقْنَاكُم مِّن قَبْلِ أَن يَأْتِيَ يَوْمٌ لَّا بَيْعٌ فِيهِ وَلَاخُلَّةٌ وَلَا شَفَاعَةٌ وَالْكَافِرُونَ هُمُ الظَّالِمُونَ

"Oh you who believe! Spend of that with which We have provided for you, before a Day comes when there will be no bargaining, nor friendship, nor intercession. And it is the disbelievers who are the wrongdoers."
(Sūrah al-Baqarah, 2:263)

Ibn al-Qayyim (ﷺ) said:

"Ward off the (evil) passing thought, for if you do not do that, it will become an idea. Ward off the idea, for if you do not do that it will become a desire. Then fight it, for if you do not do that it will become a resolve and ambition, and if you do not ward that off it will become an action. If you do not counter it with its opposite, it will become a habit, and then it will be difficult for you to get rid of it." (Al-Fawaa'id)

We must resist these whispers and passing thoughts lest they trigger our nafs and the problem becomes serious. We must especially be cautious in this matter because even if we are able to curb or control our desires in the beginning, the more we are exposed to it over time, the more we will want to persist in it. Once the nafs starts dwelling on these desires, it remains strong in its stand. Like a stubborn child, it will insist that its wishes be fulfilled right away. It will not budge until it gets what it wants and hardly ever accepts a substitute.

Shaytān withdraws at the moment we remain firm on our path to Allah, paying no attention to every whim of our desires.

Furthermore, Shaytān adds fuel to these weaknesses of the nafs. He is never inattentive about our vulnerability and always on the move, doing whatever it takes to ruin our faith. Any desires detrimental to our faith, whether it be music, sexual temptations, lying, stealing, unrestrained anger, envy, or pride should be stopped at the very first instance, lest they become a habit and lead to our ruin.

6.3.2 The nafs is self-delusional

Another danger of the nafs is that it is self-delusional. It expects rewards and praises without even working for them.

Yahya ibn Mu'ādh (ﷺ) said,

"In my opinion, the worst kind of self-delusion is for someone to sin excessively and then to hope for forgiveness without feeling any remorse; or it is to expect to draw near to Allah, the Exalted, without obeying or worshipping Him; or it is to hope for the fruits of the Garden after having only planted the seeds for the Fire; or it is to seek the abode of the obedient through committing wrong actions; or it is to expect a reward after having done nothing worthwhile; or it is to place hope in Allah, Glorious and Mighty is He, after having exceeded all the limits." (Rawdat al-'uqalā' wa nuzhat al-fudalā', Ibn Hibban)

6.3.3 Insān doesn't like to toil

The nafs, by its very nature, does not like to toil. It wants to have fun, remain lazy, and seeks instant gratification, thereby engaging in self-deception. It presents justifications and excuses to silence our conscience (nafs al-Lawwāmah) by saying things like, "everyone is doing it, so you can too", "you're not in the mood now, so do it tomorrow", "you're so busy, you've got other things to do", "you can't focus now, so continue later", "chill today, relax, have fun", "don't do anything important", "check your social media/email just one more time," etc.

Such excuses slacken and slow us down in life, whereby we end up getting distracted and wasting the valuable opportunities that lay ahead of us.

What is the solution?

Simply put, the solution lies in training the nafs and in building the spiritual strength of our heart. This is Mujāhidah, striving and struggling against one's nafs. It is like mastering a game; practice makes perfect.

So, when Shaytān and our nafs try to stop us from doing something good, we should resolve to simply do it. Tell your nafs and Shaytān, "I am going to work on this project and not get distracted as it helps me get closer to Allah"; "I am going to call my parents right now instead of delaying it until I'm free, as that time won't come"; "I will not neglect my kids, rather I will take out time to spend with them"; "I will not lie to get the job I need desperately"; "I will not take interest to fulfil my needs and desires," etc.

Remember that it is the struggle that Allah rewards. He recompenses us based on our intentions, actions, and the efforts we put in, not the results that come about. Whether we intend to get married, write a book, start a business, do tarbiyah of our children, or perform any work of goodness, we need to do our part in dodging the whispers of Shaytān and training our nafs to resist them, all the while asking Allah to create ease.

وَٱلَّذِينَ جَٰهَدُواْ فِينَا لَنَهۡدِيَنَّهُمۡ سُبُلَنَاۚ ٦٩

"And those who strive for Our sake, We will most certainly show them our paths." (Sūrah al-'Ankabūt , 29:69)

Nurturing and training our nafs is not as difficult as it seems. Consider the lengths a person would go to for the sake of his physical well-being. If one is told he has cholesterol or diabetes, he would make desperate efforts to improve his condition, like taking regular walks, medications, and dietary precautions to keep it under control. If physical health can thrive with training and determination, so can spiritual health. But for that we need to practice Mujāhidah.

Keep in Mind

Mujāhidah means 'to struggle towards training the nafs'. It is a purposeful, beneficial struggle to overcome difficulty; and it refers to the last part of our struggle. It is this part of our struggle that brings us immense joy because we overcame our weakness. We can make an effort and start with little things in order to fight our weakness.

Every person has to strive against himself.
Take, for example, the case of a man who:

→ Upon hearing the call to prayer, gets up and aims to beat the others to the mosque though he feels lazy.

→ Fulfils the sunnah prayers to the best of his abilities though his work awaits him.

→ Recites the Quran, memorizes from it as per his capacity, learns it through authentic scholars, tries to act on its teaching, ponders over its verses, and then passes it on to others.

→ Stops himself from telling lies, gossiping, and talking bad about others, though he is tempted to give in.

→ Sets his heart free from greed, love of wealth, and worldly grandeur by giving in charity from what he loves and desires, even though he dislikes parting with his hard-earned money.

وَأَنفِقُوا خَيْرًا لِّأَنفُسِكُمْ

"And spend because that is what is best for yourselves."

(Sūrah at-Taghabun, 64:16)

These examples, although seemingly mundane, are the epitome of what is called 'Mujāhidah'.

When harm overcomes us from an external enemy - for example, our wealth is usurped or our honor is violated - then Allah (ﷻ) will expiate some of our sins and raise our status. But this is not the case when it comes to being overpowered by our nafs because the nafs can only overcome us by desiring that which is forbidden and that which will lead to our disgrace and a severe punishment in this world and the Hereafter.

Therefore, the sensible one will be more cautious of his nafs and strive harder against it than striving against an enemy who is after his wealth, honor, or life.

This is how our Prophet (ﷺ) disciplined us in various ahadīth, referring to a mujāhid as the one who strives against his nafs in obedience to Allah Almighty in times of both ease and hardship.

"The one who strives in the way of Allah, the Exalted, is he who strives against his nafs." (Musnad Ahmad)

When we make this striving an ongoing process throughout our lives, we will receive incredible glad tidings on the Day of Judgement.

وَأَمَّا مَنْ خَافَ مَقَامَ رَبِّهِۦ وَنَهَى ٱلنَّفْسَ عَنِ ٱلْهَوَىٰ ﴿٤٠﴾
فَإِنَّ ٱلْجَنَّةَ هِىَ ٱلْمَأْوَىٰ ﴿٤١﴾

"And as for whoever feared to stand before his Lord and restrained the desires of his self. Then indeed, Paradise will be [his] refuge." (Sūrah an-Nazi'āt, 79:40-41)

Allah gives glad tidings of Paradise for one whose nafs al-Ammārah Bissu' (self which commands evil) encourages him to sin, yet he curbs it out of fear of standing in front of his Rabb.

The awareness that nothing at all escapes Allah Almighty and He has full knowledge of all that mankind does, pushes one to do acts of obedience to Allah and remain steadfast on the Straight Path. This can be achieved by:

i. Attaching sincerity to your actions;

ii. Continuously seeking Allah's guidance whenever you feel lost and confused.

iii. Taking every opportunity to do good that comes your way, however insignificant.

iv. Refuting the desires of the nafs, never allowing it to feel secure from Allah's respite.

We ask Allah, the Exalted, Lord of the great Throne, that He make us from those whose eternal abode will be Paradise. Aameen.

Chapter 7

A Blessing in Disguise: True Striving

اللَّهُمَّ إِنِّي أَعُوذُ بِكَ مِنْ جَهْدِ الْبَلَاءِ
وَدَرَكِ الشَّقَاءِ، وَسُوءِ الْقَضَاءِ، وَشَمَاتَةِ الْأَعْدَاءِ

Oh Allah, I seek refuge in You from severe calamity,
from misery to fall upon me, from misfortune
in the decree, and from the joys of the enemies.
(Sahīh al-Bukhari)

Our biggest struggle lies in resisting against the temptations of our nafs. But by undergoing this struggle, it is we alone who stand to benefit from its monumental results.

The Prophet (ﷺ) said,

"Paradise is surrounded by hardships and Hellfire is surrounded by temptations." (Sahīh al-Bukhari)

Imām an-Nawawi (رحمه الله), in his commentary on this hadīth in Sahīh Muslim, said:

"We can only access Jannah by performing what is widely considered as hardship (like exerting efforts in worship, being patient, doing good deeds, offering sadaqah, restraining anger, pardoning others, being good to people who have wronged us, etc.). Whereas, access to Jahannam is basically easy as one just needs to follow his nafs and desires. That is why the term 'temptations' was used."

When we wholeheartedly believe that whatever Allah decrees is the best for us, i.e., whatever He commands is for our benefit, and whatever He forbids is detrimental for us, it will:

→ Help us curb our desires, even if we love them, solely because Allah forbade it.

→ Make us be immersed in acts of obedience and righteousness (like making du'a, doing dhikr, seeking knowledge, performing salāh, etc.) such that eventually we start finding pleasure in doing them.

→ Bring discipline into our lives and make us productive by removing unnecessary distractions from our everyday routine.

The more we believe in this fact, the more readily we will accept His laws to be a means of nurturing for us, and the faster our progression will be towards Him.

يَٰٓأَيُّهَا ٱلْإِنسَٰنُ إِنَّكَ كَادِحٌ إِلَىٰ رَبِّكَ كَدْحًا فَمُلَٰقِيهِ ﴿٦﴾

"O mankind, indeed, you are laboring towards your Lord with (great) exertion and will (eventually) meet it [i.e., the consequences]."
(Sūrah al-Inshiqāq, 84:6)

7.1 Why is life so difficult?

Why would Allah put us through tests if He loves us so much? Life is not a bed of roses. Allah tells us in the Quran that every human being is constantly struggling in this life, regardless of his belief and deeds. Why is that so?

To understand this better, let us take day to day life examples.

Example 1:

When in school, all students must go through examinations to prove that they meet the criteria to move on to the next level. One might wonder how ruthless a teacher can be to make helpless students go through such an ordeal. Why doesn't the teacher let them all pass with flying colors and say, "I love you all so much, everybody gets an A"?

No teacher who truly loves her students would do this. Most children do not like to study but they have to because they need to pass the test. They cannot make it through without studying and preparing for the exam.

Then, when the exam paper is structured, it comprises of questions which are mostly generic and easily doable. But the teacher deliberately throws in a couple of difficult questions to filter out the high achievers. So, the purpose of the exam is not to unnecessarily burden the students, rather it is to gauge the level of each student (who is excelling, who is an average student, and who is below average) so as to provide appropriate help and expertise to each.

To Allah alone belongs the best of examples. When Allah puts us through trials and tribulations in life it is only to elevate us. For some, the trials are more difficult than for others according to our level of faith in Him and His decree.

Example 2:

To explain further why we are put to test, imagine a person who joins a weightlifting fitness regime.

As a beginner, it is difficult for him to work with even a lightweight dumbbell and he gets breathless while struggling to lift heavier weights. But his trainer motivates him and gradually keeps increasing the weights from one kilogram to five, to ten, and more. He keeps pushing the trainee within his capacity because he knows he can do it. The trainer, by no means, enjoys putting his trainee through so much pain.

By willingly accepting all this struggle, the trainee is not doing any favors for the trainer either. Rather, it is the other way around. With every session, the trainee's stamina increases and he becomes stronger and fitter. Yes, it is strenuous, but with steadfastness and persistence he eventually achieves his goal.

Similarly, with every trial, we come out stronger if we go through it with patience. It may appear hard, but through it, not only will the 'high achievers' emerge, but also everyone who surpasses the tests will get spiritually stronger, tougher, and better. These trials are there to purify us into becoming better people, better Muslims.

So yes, life is hard because we did not come into this world just to relax. The ultimate relief and relaxation will only come once we step into Paradise.

جَنَّٰتُ عَدۡنٖ يَدۡخُلُونَهَا يُحَلَّوۡنَ فِيهَا مِنۡ أَسَاوِرَ مِن ذَهَبٖ وَلُؤۡلُؤٗاۖ وَلِبَاسُهُمۡ فِيهَا حَرِيرٞ ٣٣

وَقَالُواْ ٱلۡحَمۡدُ لِلَّهِ ٱلَّذِيٓ أَذۡهَبَ عَنَّا ٱلۡحَزَنَۖ إِنَّ رَبَّنَا لَغَفُورٞ شَكُورٌ ٣٤

ٱلَّذِيٓ أَحَلَّنَا دَارَ ٱلۡمُقَامَةِ مِن فَضۡلِهِۦ لَا يَمَسُّنَا فِيهَا نَصَبٞ وَلَا يَمَسُّنَا فِيهَا لُغُوبٞ ٣٥

"And (Eden) Paradise (everlasting Gardens) will they enter. Therein will they be adorned with bracelets of gold and pearls, and their garments there will be of silk. And they (the believers) will say: 'All the praises and thanks be to Allah, who has removed from us (all) grief. Verily, our Lord is indeed Oft-Forgiving, Most Appreciative (good deeds and to recompense). Who, out of His Grace, has lodged us in a home that will last forever. There, neither toil will touch us, nor weariness.'"
(Sūrah Fatir, 35:33-35)

Ahead of us is an abode of happiness that is everlasting and also one of punishment that is everlasting. It is an abode where we will reap the consequences of our actions in this world. We must strive for the abode that has eternal bliss and fear the life of eternal punishment. No matter how difficult life gets, we have to keep going because this life is temporary. Its pleasures and sadness, its good and its evils, its poverty and its riches - all of it is temporary.

Allah, the All-Wise, knows what we need in order to be purified and upgraded to Jannah. He knows what we require to reform - whether it is advice from a book, a sentence, a word, a person, or from a source we never expected. Allah Almighty guides different people to different resources in order to perfect their faith. Everyone is on their own unique journey.

At the end of it all, our goal should be to attain Paradise, the everlasting life with permanent delights. That would be the place we can finally relax and get all of our heart's desires.

7.2 Wisdom behind Trials

Some of the wisdom behind Allah choosing to make us go through trials and difficulties may include the following reasons:

7.2.1 To earn Allah's love

As counterintuitive as it may seem, Allah gives us tests only out of His love for us. The Prophet (ﷺ) said,

"When Allah loves a servant, He tests him." (Sunan at-Tirmidhī)

In fact, Allah's jabr (mending) is one of the greatest blessings we can receive.

In a hadīth qudsī, Allah Almighty tells Angel Jibreel (عليه السلام) to delay the response to the du'a of a servant because He Almighty loves hearing His servant's voice. (at-Tabarani)

Sometimes the reason to be put through hardships, loss, and pain, is to grant us the sweetness of conversing with Allah, the Most Loving, to spend long hours in the night beseeching Him through tears of sincerity.

7.2.2 To guide us to our purpose

We have an important objective in this life—to worship Allah Almighty alone. He Almighty nūrtures us through seemingly difficult times to make this path easy for us, by bringing us out of the darkness of shirk and disobedience into the light of tawhīd (i.e., worshipping Allah alone) and obedience, thus bringing us closer to Him.

7.2.3 To purify us

Tests and calamities are a means by which Allah expiates sins in this world. The Prophet (ﷺ) said,

"No fatigue, nor disease, nor sorrow, nor sadness, nor hurt, nor distress befalls a Muslim, even if it were the prick he receives from a thorn, except that Allah expiates some of his sins for it." (Sahīh al-Bukhari)

With every test, Allah wants to purify, nurture, and elevate us to be worthy of Paradise.

Our ultimate aim is to earn Allah's pleasure and Jannah, yet we fall short in worshipping Allah Almighty as He should be worshiped. Many of us have shortcomings in our acts of worship (such as salāh, sawm, etc.), and we fail to ask for forgiveness regularly or to reflect on our state and return to Allah Almighty. These tests, as burdensome as they are, make up for those shortcomings and ease our burden on the Day of Judgment, if we respond with patience.

"The most prone to trials are Prophets, then the most pious, and then the less pious." (Sahīh al-Bukhari)

This tells us that the closer a person is to Allah in righteousness and steadfastness, the more that he will be tested.

Let us recall the difficulties Prophet (ﷺ) faced from the time he came to this world. From being born as an orphan, to losing his parents and guardian in childhood, to facing severe persecutions whilst spreading the message of Allah, to losing his most loved ones - his beloved wife, Khadija (رضي الله عنها) and his uncle Abu Talib, who were two of his strongest supporters during the most crucial time of his life, as well as his children. He definitely felt sorrow and expressed his emotions through tears and grief. Yet he (ﷺ) dealt with every affliction with dignity, maintaining his boundaries with Allah, the most Loving, and hoping the best from Him. At the death of his son Ibrahīm, he wept and said,

"The eyes are shedding tears and the heart is grieved, but we will not say except what pleases our Lord. Oh Ibrahīm! Indeed, we are grieved by your separation." (Sahīh al-Bukhari)

A test does not always mean a loss or trying times, but it can be presented as a blessing too. How does a person react towards his good fortune? Does he attribute his success to himself (thus failing the test) or does he humble himself in gratitude towards his Creator and use his blessings to earn His pleasure (hence passing the test)?

7.2.4 To filter the truthful ones from the rest

This world is our examination hall, and this is where we will be answering our tests to reap the benefits in the Hereafter. As we move on with life, with each passing test, the subsequent appraisals become more challenging to see how high we can climb and to establish our quality. Allah Almighty knows our capacity and is fully aware of our struggles too. He will never test us beyond our capacity.

But the test needs to happen.

وَلَقَدْ فَتَنَّا ٱلَّذِينَ مِن قَبْلِهِمْ ۖ فَلَيَعْلَمَنَّ ٱللَّهُ ٱلَّذِينَ صَدَقُوا۟ وَلَيَعْلَمَنَّ ٱلْكَـٰذِبِينَ ﴿٣﴾

"And We indeed tested those who were before them. And Allah will certainly make (it) known (the truth of) those who are true and will certainly make (it) known (the falsehood of) those who are liars, (although Allah knows all that before putting them to test)."
(Sūrah al-'Ankabūt , 29:3)

This world, an abode of tests and trials, is a place for us to work hard and strive in so we can get into the high-achieving crowd, be filtered to the top ranks, and hence be rewarded accordingly. Our outcome will depend on how well we cope with our hardships.

So, take for instance a mother who lost her child. How will she face this extremely difficult trial? She may scream, refuse to accept reality, and curse the divine decree, or she may go into a catatonic state, giving up entirely. These kinds of reactions imply failing the test that Allah placed her in. She may then face wrath from her Lord and, as a result, humiliation in the life of this world.

But if she chooses to exercise sabr (patience) by accepting the decree in her heart and on her lips, constantly declaring al-hamdulillāh, then she would have used her situation as an opportunity to elevate her position in the sight of Allah. If she considered her child as an amānah from Allah, reminding herself that Allah is the one true Owner of her child, and she displayed no negative reactions even though she was grieved by her great loss, then she has surely used this tough situation to earn herself a great reward.

In such a case, Allah promises the mother an increase and a beautiful recompense. Perhaps Allah, the Provider, will replace her with a better child in this world and elevate her ranks in the Hereafter or perhaps her baby will intercede for her salvation on the Day of Judgement.

Similarly, consider a person who is tested with the promotion he fervently desired at his workplace. Does he regard this blessing as a gift from Allah and increase in his gratitude towards Him, or does he attribute the promotion to his own talents, experiences, and knowledge, forgetting that it was Allah who decreed it to happen in the first place? If he regarded the promotion as a blessing, then he has passed the test and is promised increment because of his gratitude. Whereas he would have failed the test if he attributed the achievement to his own self, not thanking or praising Allah in the process, and thereby having put himself in a vulnerable situation both in this world and the Hereafter.

وَمَا يَسْتَوِى ٱلْأَعْمَىٰ وَٱلْبَصِيرُ وَٱلَّذِينَ ءَامَنُوا۟ وَعَمِلُوا۟ ٱلصَّـٰلِحَـٰتِ
وَلَا ٱلْمُسِىٓءُ ۚ قَلِيلًا مَّا تَتَذَكَّرُونَ ﴿٥٨﴾

"And not equal are the blind and those who see, nor are (equal) those who believe (in the oneness of Allah and Islamic monotheism) and do righteous good deeds, and those who do evil. Little do you remember."
(Sūrah Ghāfır, 40:58)

7.2.5 To show us where we stand

Hard times don't stay forever, but they do show us our true colors. Do we come closer to Allah Almighty only in times of ease or does our trust in Him extend to times of hardship as well? When we are tested, do we abandon the good deeds that we used to do or do we hold onto them firmer than ever before? Allah Almighty describes such people in the following verse:

وَمِنَ ٱلنَّاسِ مَن يَعْبُدُ ٱللَّهَ عَلَىٰ حَرْفٍۖ فَإِنْ أَصَابَهُۥ
خَيْرٌ ٱطْمَأَنَّ بِهِۦۖ وَإِنْ أَصَابَتْهُ فِتْنَةٌ ٱنقَلَبَ عَلَىٰ وَجْهِهِۦ
خَسِرَ ٱلدُّنْيَا وَٱلْءَاخِرَةَۚ ذَٰلِكَ هُوَ ٱلْخُسْرَانُ ٱلْمُبِينُ ﴿١١﴾

"And of the people is he who worships Allah on an edge. If he is touched by good, he is reassured by it; but if he is struck by trial, he turns on his face (to the other direction). He has lost (this) world and the Hereafter. That is what is the manifest loss."
(Sūrah al-Hajj, 22:11)

If our worth is of '22 karat gold', Allah wants to increase our worth to that of '24 karat gold' by showing us where we stand through the realization of:

- Our weaknesses, so we know what we need to work on, and
- Our potentials, so we expand our boundaries.

7.2.6 To make us appreciate the importance of Allah's favors

أَمْ حَسِبْتُمْ أَن تَدْخُلُوا۟ ٱلْجَنَّةَ وَلَمَّا يَأْتِكُم مَّثَلُ ٱلَّذِينَ خَلَوْا۟ مِن قَبْلِكُمۖ
مَّسَّتْهُمُ ٱلْبَأْسَآءُ وَٱلضَّرَّآءُ وَزُلْزِلُوا۟ حَتَّىٰ يَقُولَ ٱلرَّسُولُ وَٱلَّذِينَ ءَامَنُوا۟ مَعَهُۥ
مَتَىٰ نَصْرُ ٱللَّهِۗ أَلَآ إِنَّ نَصْرَ ٱللَّهِ قَرِيبٌ ﴿٢١٤﴾

"Or do you think that you will enter Paradise without such (trials) as came to those who passed away before you? They were afflicted with severe poverty and ailments and were

so shaken that even the Messenger and those who believed along with him said, 'When will the help of Allah arrive?' Unquestionably, indeed the help of Allah is near"
(Sūrah al-Baqarah, 2:214)

Ibn al-Qayyim (ﷺ) said:

"This is from the perfection of the Lord's favors and blessings that He Almighty makes His slave taste the bitterness of being broken down into fragments before making him taste the sweetness of relief and reparation. Allah Almighty makes the person know the extent of His favors upon him by testing him with the opposite (i.e., by taking away the favors). Like the time He Almighty wished to complete for Adam (ﷺ) the pleasure and delight of Paradise. He was made to taste the bitterness of being expelled from Jannah and suffering in this abode (earth), in which prosperity and pleasure are blended in with hardships and tribulations.

So, He Almighty does not 'break' His believing slave except to mend him, and He Almighty does not prevent from him except to give it to him, and He Almighty does not afflict him (with sickness) except to heal him, and He Almighty does not cause him to die except to resurrect him, and He Almighty does not constrict for him the world except to make him yearn more for the Hereafter, and He Almighty does not test him with people's rudeness except to make him turn towards Him Almighty". (Mukhtasar as-sawā'iq al-Mursalah)

This realization, however, will come only to a believer—one who is struggling for the sake of His Lord, who he believes will, without a doubt, reform him and compensate him generously on the Final Day. It is important to know this perspective because we do not want to look at our life and just feel pain.

Take for instance the hardship and struggle that Prophet Yūsuf (ﷺ) had to undergo. As a child, he was separated from his loving father by his own brothers due to their jealousy. He went from living a secure life under his doting father to being forced to live the life of a slave. Later, in his youth, he was accused of evil doings that he did not perpetrate and was thrown into prison for many years to curb the wild desires of the women of the city. Though these trials seemed difficult and unfair, they turned out to be blessings in disguise. Every situation he faced in life eventually led to his elevation of becoming the minister of Egypt. With every adversity, Allah was nurturing him to be worthy of this position.

Every decree in life, past or present that may be extremely difficult to bear, is actually beneficial for us. When we realize this fact it:

Becomes easier for us to be patient.

Gives us comfort and makes us pleased with Allah's decree.

Makes us grateful for any situation, even a small and insignificant one.

Allah will not put us through calamities and then leave us alone without giving us the tools to succeed in those tests. In fact, ours is an open-book test with the answers clearly marked.

We must always keep in mind that Allah, the All-Wise, intends to nurture and reform us so that we become deserving of entering His vicinity in Paradise. Not every slave is worthy of this immense reward. Only the one who accepts Allah's method of nurturing with a pure heart will earn it.

May Allah Almighty help us to accept our nurturing and elevate us through it. Aameen.

Chapter 8

What You Sow, You Shall Reap

رَبِّ هَبْ لِي حُكْمًا وَأَلْحِقْنِى بِٱلصَّـٰلِحِينَ

My Lord, grant me authority and join me with the righteous. (Sūrah ash-Shu'arā, 26:83)

Has it ever happened that one sowed a seed of a cactus and it grew a tomato plant? Never. What we sow is what will come out. When the heart is sown with the 'seeds' of the Quran, adhkār, and eemān-building lectures, its 'produce' would most likely be righteous good deeds, as our actions are a manifestation of what is in our hearts. Furthermore, the more sincere our deeds are, the closer we will get to Allah.

Likewise, Shaytān and our nafs intend to sow seeds of evil and negativity within our hearts. Time after time, they will keep irrigating these seeds, until they turn into intentions. They will continue engaging with us until our intentions become firm resolutions and the resolutions yield actions. These evil thoughts planted into the heart by the nafs and Shaytān will, in turn, gradually overcome thoughts of faith, love, and turning repentantly to Allah. This is why repelling evil thoughts is easier than repelling intentions and firm resolutions.

The heart can settle down only with one of two types of thoughts—good or bad. It will retain the one that is stronger and expel the one that is weaker.

So, we must work on guarding and protecting our heart from thoughts that will corrupt it.

The Messenger of Allah (ﷺ) said,

"There are four kinds of hearts: a polished heart as shiny as a radiant lamp, a sealed heart with a knot tied around it, a heart that is turned upside down, and a heart that is wrapped. As for the polished heart, it is the heart of the believer and its lamp is the light of faith. The sealed heart is the heart of the unbeliever. The heart that is turned upside down is the heart of a pure hypocrite, for he had knowledge but he denied it. As for the heart that is wrapped, it is the heart that contains both faith and hypocrisy. The parable of faith in this heart is the parable of the herb that is sustained by pure water, and the parable of the hypocrisy in it is the parable of an ulcer that thrives upon pus and blood; whichever of the two is greater will dominate." (Musnad Ahmad)

What we choose to grow is in our hands: either herbs, which are beneficial to all, or ulcers, which are harmful and painful. Whichever of them prevails in our nafs is what will dominate the outcome of our character and behavior.

8.1 The choice is ours:

We give in to our desires and fall prey to the whispers of Shaytān.	OR	We struggle against his whispers and live according to the teachings of Islam with dignity and respect.
We irrigate our hearts with the temptations of this world.	OR	We irrigate our heart with the Nūr (light) of eeman.
We choose to be affected with the pomp and glitter of this world (like wealth, recognition, fame, kids, powerful positions, etc.), all of which are temporary.	OR	We remain focused on the Hereafter, which is an everlasting reality.
We choose to be deluded by the distractions of this world.	OR	We are constantly aware of Allah and frequently remember His presence.
We let this world derail us from the Straight Path.	OR	We stay focused on the Straight Path, both in our 'ibadāt (acts of worship) as well as our mu'amalāt (day-to-day dealings).
We choose Paradise.	OR	We choose Hellfire.

We alone will be held responsible for the choices we make, as that is what will define our success or failure in this world and the Hereafter. This world is where we sow and the Hereafter is where we will reap.

ٱلۡيَوۡمَ تُجۡزَىٰ كُلُّ نَفۡسِۭ بِمَا كَسَبَتۡۚ لَا ظُلۡمَ ٱلۡيَوۡمَۚ إِنَّ ٱللَّهَ سَرِيعُ ٱلۡحِسَابِ ﴿١٧﴾

"This Day every person shall be recompensed for what he earned. No injustice (shall be done to anybody). Truly, Allah is swift in reckoning."
(Sūrah Ghāfir, 40:17)

قُلۡ كُلّٞ يَعۡمَلُ عَلَىٰ شَاكِلَتِهِۦ فَرَبُّكُمۡ أَعۡلَمُ بِمَنۡ هُوَ أَهۡدَىٰ سَبِيلٗا ﴿٨٤﴾

"Say (O Muhammad to mankind): 'Each one does according to his way [i.e., his religion, intentions, etc.] and your Lord knows best of him whose path is right.'"
(Sūrah al-Isrā', 17:84)

Our nafs is waiting to be led towards the light. We are not here on a useless or random trip. Each and every one of us has a mission to serve in the servitude of Allah Almighty. We need to live up to it and leave a legacy behind us.

8.2 Seeking Allah's help through Quranic tools

In order to carry out this mission, we need the help of our Creator. His reforming is in the most subtle manner, nurturing us through the most eloquent and clearest of statements - the Quran, the final Book of Allah. All that is in it is true. No falsehood can be attached to it. It tells us everything clearly and truthfully and serves as the ultimate guide for our lives.

يَٰٓأَيُّهَا ٱلنَّاسُ قَدۡ جَآءَتۡكُم مَّوۡعِظَةٞ مِّن رَّبِّكُمۡ
وَشِفَآءٞ لِّمَا فِي ٱلصُّدُورِ وَهُدٗى وَرَحۡمَةٞ لِّلۡمُؤۡمِنِينَ ﴿٥٧﴾

"O mankind! There has come to you a good advice from your Lord and a healing for that which is in your breasts (disease of ignorance, doubt, hypocrisy and differences, etc.), a guidance, and a mercy (explaining lawful and unlawful things, etc.) for the believers."
(Sūrah Yūnus, 10:57)

Through the Quran, Allah, our Creator, guides us step by step, provides us with a means of protection from our enemies, removes our confusions, solves conflicts amongst us, and keeps us steadfast on the Straight Path.

Quranic tools in order to be firm in our servitude to Allah.

8.2.1 Holding on to the Quran

وَٱتْلُ مَآ أُوحِىَ إِلَيْكَ مِن كِتَابِ رَبِّكَ ۖ
لَا مُبَدِّلَ لِكَلِمَٰتِهِۦ وَلَن تَجِدَ مِن دُونِهِۦ مُلْتَحَدًا ﴿٢٧﴾

"And recite what has been revealed to you of the Book of your Lord (i.e., recite it, understand it, follow its teachings, act on its orders, and preach it to men). None can change His Words, and none will you find as a refuge other than Him." (Sūrah al-Kahf, 18:27)

Nothing will help us decide the best course of action other than the Quran.

The only way to conquer our two biggest enemies, Shaytān and the nafs, is to live according to the teachings of the Quran. We need to put in all the necessary efforts to understand the Quran so as to appreciate the wisdom in it and obtain endless guidance from it.

To understand the Quran:

We can begin by reading an authentic translation of the Quran in English (Sahīh International is highly recommended by scholars) or any language that we understand fluently.

It is also important to reflect and ponder upon the verses that we are reading. Taking the aid of authentic tafasīr (scholarly explanations of the Quranic text) will help us ponder by deepening our knowledge.

Most importantly, we need to set our intentions right - why we are reading the Quran, and what we want to get out of it - even before we start reading.

The one and only ilāh and Creator of everything sent this Quran for humans and jinns in all times and all places, but especially for those who have intellect, to show us the purpose of our life and how we must live it in order to fulfil that purpose. Allah says in the Quran,

كِتَٰبٌ أَنزَلْنَٰهُ إِلَيْكَ مُبَٰرَكٌ لِّيَدَّبَّرُوٓاْ ءَايَٰتِهِۦ
وَلِيَتَذَكَّرَ أُوْلُواْ ٱلْأَلْبَٰبِ ﴿٢٩﴾

"(This is) a blessed Book which We have revealed to you, (O Muhammad), that they might reflect upon its verses and that those of understanding would be reminded."
(Sūrah Sād, 38:29)

8.2.2 Holding on to the dīn

وَٱصْبِرْ نَفْسَكَ مَعَ ٱلَّذِينَ يَدْعُونَ رَبَّهُم بِٱلْغَدَوٰةِ وَٱلْعَشِيِّ يُرِيدُونَ وَجْهَهُۥ
وَلَا تَعْدُ عَيْنَاكَ عَنْهُمْ تُرِيدُ زِينَةَ ٱلْحَيَوٰةِ ٱلدُّنْيَا وَلَا تُطِعْ مَنْ أَغْفَلْنَا قَلْبَهُۥ
عَن ذِكْرِنَا وَٱتَّبَعَ هَوَىٰهُ وَكَانَ أَمْرُهُۥ فُرُطًا ﴿٢٨﴾

"And keep yourself (O Muhammad) patiently with those who call on their Lord (i.e., your companions who remember their Lord with glorification, praising in prayers, etc., and other righteous deeds) morning and afternoon, seeking His Face. And let not your eyes overlook them, desiring the pomp and glitter of the life of the world, and obey not him whose heart We have made heedless of Our remembrance, one who follows his own lusts and whose affair (deeds) has been lost."
(Sūrah al-Kahf, 18:28)

No matter how overpowering or difficult our situation may be, we need to patiently hold on to our dīn, without compromising our values or adopting the herd mentality. Being brave and doing the right thing even when we are the only ones following the right path is what will make us special to Allah. When we are unable to change the situation we are in, we must never lose hope, and instead, patiently hold onto the rope of Allah. This is sabr to hang on with dignity until

Allah Almighty, out of His perfect wisdom, decides to lift our problems off our shoulders and make things easy for us.

We may not have the power to change our circumstances, but Allah surely can. So, we must trust in Him, and find solace in:

i. The promise of Allah, the Most Truthful, when He says, "He, the Almighty, will not allow to be lost the reward of any who did well in deeds." (Sūrah al-Kahf, 18:30)

ii. The beautiful advice by Sufyān ath-Thawrī (ﷺ) that encourages us to stay away from difficult situations and hold on to our dīn:

"Improve your secret and private life, and Allah will improve your public and social life. Make matters well between you and Allah, and Allah will make matters well between you and the people. Work for the Hereafter and Allah will be enough for you in your worldly concerns." (The Biography of Sufyan ath-Thawrī)

iii. The du'a that the Prophet (ﷺ) taught us to say when in distress:

اللّهُـمَّ رَحْمَتَـكَ أَرْجـوفَلا تَكِلـني إِلى نَفْـسي طَـرْفَةَ عَـيْن
وَأَصْلِـحْ لي شَأْنـي كُلَّـه لا إِلَهَ إِلاّ أَنْـت

Allāhumma rahmataka arjoo fa laa takilni ilaa nafsi tarfat 'ayn, wa aslih li sha'ni kullahu, laa ilaaha illa anta

Oh Allah, for Your mercy I hope, so do not leave me in charge of my affairs even for the blink of an eye. Rectify all my affairs. There is no deity except You. (Sunan Abu Dawūd)

8.2.3 Holding on to the way of the righteous ones

We must avoid hanging around with people whose hearts are consumed by this world and are void of Allah's remembrance—those who blindly follow their desires and live a life based on 'me, myself, and I'. They believe in what they call the YOLO ('you only live once') lifestyle and do whatever their hearts desire. They fail to think that if we are going to 'only live once', wouldn't that be even more of a reason to make the most of this life to invest in the eternal abode of the Hereafter?

Such a crowd is the worst one to be with. We must maintain our distance from them so as not to be influenced by them. After all, friendship is not only a social need. Rather, it also plays a significant role in our lives because of the enormous influence it has on us. The Prophet (ﷺ) advised us:

"A man follows the religion of his friend so each one should consider whom he makes his friend." (Sunan Abu Dawūd)

We need to keep friends who bring us closer to Allah. To find such friends we will have to take effective practical steps, starting with making du'a to Allah Almighty to grant us righteous companionship and a better replacement for whom we leave for His sake.

Practical steps towards finding righteous companionship

The first thing we should do is try to make our existing friendships purposeful by being the type of friend that gets others closer to Allah.

If we find that we do not have righteous people around us, then we should try to create a virtuous environment by being a good role model ourselves. We must avoid stressing out if, even after trying very hard, we are unable to find righteous friends, as Allah does not expect from us anything beyond our capacity.

Also, it may be that despite having several Muslim friends, we happen to be closest to the one who neglects their prayers and has others major vices. In such a case, it is incumbent upon us to advise them to start following the teachings of Islam, and if that doesn't work, we have to limit our interactions with them.

Secondly, we should constantly seek avenues where we will meet righteous people—be it at local mosques or Islamic talks and study circles.

These efforts on our part show that we are serious in trying to follow the advice of the Prophet (ﷺ) and, by the Will of Allah, He will grant us righteous company and friends who remind us of our purpose and our Rabb. The owner of all hearts can surely bring us closer to hearts that remember Him often.

8.2.4 Du'a with sincerity

Du'a is an essential tool in our lives which we need to hold on to even stronger during times of difficulty. When one is stuck in a cave and sees no way out, all they can do is make du'a. This is what the companions of the cave did, as mentioned in Sūrah al-Kahf. They made sincere du'a to Allah Almighty and had complete faith that He would answer.

Our du'as will be sincere when we:

1. Direct our du'as to Allah alone, continuously beseeching Him for all of our needs, while being patient and not hastening for an answer.

→ The Prophet (ﷺ) said: "The du'a of any worshiper will continue to be responded to as long as he is not hasty." It was asked, "O Messenger of Allah, what does it mean to be hasty?" He (ﷺ) responded: "A worshipper says, 'I have prayed and prayed, and I don't see that it will be accepted', so he gives up hope of his du'a being answered and leaves it altogether." (Sahīh Muslim)

2. Feel needy in front of Allah Almighty, showing our desperation to Him.

Making du'a using phrases like, "Oh Allah I need you, grant me what I am in need of, I have nowhere else to go," express our dire need for His help.

This is how Musa (عليه السلام) addressed his Rabb when he ran away from his country empty-handed out of fear of Fir'aun.

رَبِّ إِنِّى لِمَآ أَنزَلْتَ إِلَىَّ مِنْ خَيْرٍ فَقِيرٌ

Rabbi innī limā anzalta ilayya min khairin faqīr

"O my Lord! I am indeed needy of whatever good You send to me."

(Sūrah al-Qasas, 28:24)

And Allah, al-Mujīb, responded generously to his du'a by granting him not just a job thereafter but a place to stay and a family of his own.

3. Acknowledge our sins.

→ We can make du'a using words like, "Oh Allah I know I wronged myself by disobeying you. But Oh Ghafūr, you love to forgive so forgive my sins and shortcomings and give me what I need, even though I am not deserving of it. But only you can give and only you are the Giver."

Ibn al-Qayyim (رحمه الله) said, "Du'a is one of the most beneficial remedies. It is the enemy of calamity; it repels it, cures it, prevents its occurrence, and alleviates it, or reduces it if it befalls (one). It is the weapon of the believer." (ad-Dā' wal-Dawā')

8.2.5 Not desiring the pomp and glitters of this world

Our desires make living in accordance with the commands of Allah Almighty extremely difficult because they tempt us and pull us towards the luxuries and glitters of this world. We need to keep the world in our hands, use it to fulfil our requirements and free our hearts for Allah's remembrance.

The reason we fall prey to the attractions of this world is because of its addictive nature. Though not all of its attractions may be necessarily harām, they still divert us from our responsibilities and mission. Nobody starts out intending to develop an addiction, but many people get enslaved by their desires.

A few examples of modern-day addictions:

i. Immersion in playing video games

ii. Excessive shopping

iii. Disproportionate internet usage

iv. Being hooked on social media

v. Binge-watching (Netflix and the likes)

vi. Obsession with looks

vii. Constant house remodeling

viii. Fixation on cars

ix. Obsession with exercising

Addictions make us heedless so we have to work to overcome them. This requires a process that includes:

Firstly making the decision to quit the addiction and asking Allah Almighty to create ease for us.

Secondly making a solid plan to quit by:
→ Reducing the time spent on the activity.
→ Avoiding places which cause us to slip. For example, deleting or blocking online shopping sites; avoiding going to the restaurants where we tend to overindulge; and steering away from shops which tempt us to spend unnecessarily, and especially during 'sale' periods, etc.
→ Abstaining from hanging out with people who trigger the addiction.

Thirdly avoiding relapsing by:
→ Replacing the time saved from eliminating the addiction with productive therapies like understanding, memorizing, and/or reciting the Quran, listening to beneficial podcasts, reading beneficial books, and keeping in touch with loved ones.

Whatever takes us away from our 'ibādah, we must cut off. If our desires are a hindrance to our worship of Allah, we need to sacrifice them here to get whatever we yearn for in the Hereafter.

Allah reminds us time and time again that the true enjoyment is the enjoyment of Jannah. This world is a place of performing good deeds to earn Paradise by using all the possible means Allah has offered to us. He has chosen the best of divine books, the Quran, to guide us and help us achieve this. If we forsake it and seek guidance from anything other than it, we will go astray.

إِنَّآ أَنزَلۡنَا عَلَيۡكَ ٱلۡكِتَٰبَ لِلنَّاسِ بِٱلۡحَقِّۖ فَمَنِ ٱهۡتَدَىٰ فَلِنَفۡسِهِۦۖ
وَمَن ضَلَّ فَإِنَّمَا يَضِلُّ عَلَيۡهَاۖ وَمَآ أَنتَ عَلَيۡهِم بِوَكِيلٍ ﴿٤١﴾

"Verily, We have sent down upon you [O Prophet (ﷺ)] the Book (this Quran) for mankind in truth. So whosoever

accepts the guidance, it is only for his own self, and whosoever goes astray, he goes astray only for his (own) loss. And you are not a trustee over them."
(Sūrah az-Zumar, 39:41)

Our Rabb is telling us that He has sent down this Quran with the absolute truth and for the purpose of guiding us and empowering us to work towards our success and that of others.

Now it is up to us whether we accept it or reject it. Allah will never force us to accept this Quran; we decide whether we hold on to it and live by it or forsake it and neglect it. Based on our decisions, we will face our consequences - either the wrath of Allah and Hell, or His pleasure and Paradise.

Chapter 9

Empowerment with Taqwa

اللَّهُمَّ إنِّي أسألُكَ الهُدَى ، وَالتُّقَى ، وَالعَفَافَ ، وَالغِنَى

Oh Allah! I ask You for guidance, piety,
chastity, and self-sufficiency.
(Sahīh Muslim)

Allah Almighty says,

وَقُلِ ٱعْمَلُوا۟ فَسَيَرَى ٱللَّهُ عَمَلَكُمْ وَرَسُولُهُۥ
وَٱلْمُؤْمِنُونَ ۖ وَسَتُرَدُّونَ إِلَىٰ عَٰلِمِ ٱلْغَيْبِ وَٱلشَّهَٰدَةِ فَيُنَبِّئُكُم بِمَا كُنتُمْ تَعْمَلُونَ ١٠٥

"Do (as you will), for Allah will see your deeds, and (so will) His Messenger and the believers. And you will be returned to the Knower of everything hidden and apparent, and He will inform you of what you used to do."
(Sūrah at-Tawbah, 9:105)

How long are we going to give in to our desires and let our biggest enemies, Shaytān and our nafs, make us heedless of the higher purpose that we were created for? How much more are we willing to let them consume us, knowing that eventually we will be presented to our Rabb in the Hereafter when He will inform us of all that what we did?

The thought of returning to our Creator should in itself be a driving force for us to get our act together, while seeking the love and nearness of our Rabb. It should encourage us to continue doing that which is right—even when the odds are stacked against us, and no matter how difficult the struggle is.

Allah Almighty is all-aware of the purpose behind our actions. He knows whether we intended to perform a deed for His sake or if we intended it for other than Him. He is well aware of our actions even before any security camera registers our movements.

Everything we do, irrespective of how small or minute, the action and the intentions behind it are known to Allah. This implies two things:

We must never be swayed away from making progress because of a lack of appreciation. →	**Instead, we must continue progressing for the sake of Allah and, in fact, work harder and more diligently for His sake.**
We must never be satisfied with mediocrity, and we shouldn't claim self-righteousness in following just the basics of Islam simply because most other people aren't doing so. →	**Rather, we must chase after ihsān and increase the quality of our worship for the sake of Allah.**

While following one's desires can take us far away from our purpose and ultimately Allah's pleasure, taqwa will get us closer to the love of Allah.

"...For Allah loves the muttaqīn (those who have taqwa)." (Sūrah at-Tawbah, 9:4)

9.1 What is Taqwa?

9.1.1 Taqwa is to pause and think

'Is what I am doing/going to do pleasing to Allah or not?' Taqwa means to take the necessary precautions from incurring the wrath of Allah, knowing full well that the punishment of Allah is severe and that just as no one can reward like Allah, no one can punish like Him either.

Those without taqwa follow their own desires or the desires of others. They don't wish to stay within the boundaries set by Allah Almighty and have no qualms in doing or saying as their nafs pleases.

The muttaqī (one who has taqwa), on the other hand, accounts for his every deed - speech and action. He shields himself from acting or reacting in ways that are displeasing to his Rabb. He is cautious of his thoughts, utterances, and actions, and does not follow the desires of his nafs.

9.1.2 Taqwa entails us to live a life of consciousness and obedience to Allah by:

Fulfilling our obligations, and Abstaining from sins ...

...upon the Nūr (guidance) from Allah

When we live a life of obedience to Allah, viewing our worship of Him as a reminder of mercy from Allah Almighty and not as a burden or a difficulty, we will be protected from Allah's anger and His punishment.

يَـٰٓأَيُّهَا ٱلَّذِينَ ءَامَنُوا۟ ٱتَّقُوا۟ ٱللَّهَ حَقَّ تُقَاتِهِۦ وَلَا تَمُوتُنَّ إِلَّا وَأَنتُم مُّسْلِمُونَ ١٠٢

"Oh you who believe! Have taqwa of Allah, which is due to Him, and do not die unless you are Muslims." (Sūrah Āli-'Imrān, 3:102)

By living a life of taqwa, we alone stand to benefit. Our taqwa does not benefit Allah Almighty in the least bit. As our Creator, He alone knows what is suitable for us and what will safeguard us and our society. If we wish to attain His love and guidance, we must fulfil His haqq (right) of taqwa.

9.1.3 Sheikh S'adī described in his Tafsīr as-S'adī:

"The reality of taqwa is:

i. He remembers Allah and does not forget Him

ii. He obeys Allah and does not disobey Him

iii. He thanks Allah and is not ungrateful to Him"

i. To remember Allah always and never forget Him

Remembering Allah consistently will earn us Allah's pleasure and closeness. It is also a cure for all the sicknesses of the heart because the focus is on Allah Almighty rather than people and materialistic things. Living a life conscious of Allah will help us stay within the prescribed boundaries. In it, lies our happiness.

THE REMEMBRANCE OF ALLAH ENCOMPASSES:

Thinking good of Allah

Irrespective of our situation, whether we are facing a calamity or experiencing ease and comfort, it is imperative that we believe that there is wisdom behind it and that it is for our own good, even though we may not be able to comprehend it.

Moreover, good opinion of Allah must be accompanied with good speech and actions.

The Quran

Allah refers to the Quran itself as 'adh-dhikr'.

إِنْ هُوَ إِلَّا ذِكْرٌ لِّلْعَالَمِينَ

"This (the Quran) is no less than a dhikr (remembrance or reminder) for all the worlds."

(Sūrah Sād, 38:87)

→ Reading, understanding, reflecting, and pondering over Allah's Words is the most effective way of remembering Him.
→ The gatherings where people assemble to learn and teach religion and remember Him are greatly encouraged and valued in Islam.

The Prophet (ﷺ) said, "When you come upon the pastures of Paradise, feed on them." When asked what the pastures of Paradise were, he replied that they were circles where Allah is remembered. (Sunan at-Tirmidhī).

Dua (Supplications)

"Supplication is the essence of worship." (Sunan at-Tirmidhī)

Prescribed du'as from the Quran and Sunnah, as well as all other heartfelt du'as come under the banner of dhikr and form the core of worship.

Whether it is -
→ In salāh
→ At specific times when du'as are accepted like at tahajjud, between the adhān and the iqāmah, etc.
→ Any time and anything that our heart yearns to make du'a for, even for seeking a thing as simple as a new shoelace, etc.

Specified Dhikr

Such as:
→ **'Astaghfirullāh'** - Seeking Allah's forgiveness by saying "I seek Allah's forgiveness"

→ **Reciting the morning & evening adhkār**

Saying the following tasbīh:
→ **'SubhānAllāh'**- Glorifying Allah Almighty by saying, "How perfect is Allah"

→ **'Alhamdulillāh'** – Praising Him by saying, "All praise is for Allah"

→ **'SubhānAllāhi wa bihamdihi, SubhānAllāhil 'azīm'**

The Prophet (ﷺ) said: "(There are) two words (which are) light on the tongue, heavy on the Scale and beloved to the Most Gracious:

سُبْحَانَ اللهِ وَبِحَمْدِهِ،
سُبْحانَ اللهِ الْعَظِيمِ

SubhānAllāhi wa bihamdihi, SubhānAllāhil 'azīm.
(How perfect Allah is and to Him (belongs) the praise. How perfect Allah is, the Greatest.)"
(Sahīh al-Bukhari)

→ **'Lā ilāha illAllāh'** (There is no deity worthy of worship except Allah)

The Prophet (ﷺ) said, "When a servant of Allah utters the words 'Lā ilāha illAllāh' sincerely, the doors of heaven open up for these words until they reach the Throne of Allah, so long as the utterer keeps away from the major sins."
(Sunan at-Timiridhi)

→ **'Allāhu Akbar'** - Exalting Him by saying, "Allah is the Greatest"

→ **'La hawla wa la quwwata illa billah'** - (There is no power nor might except with Allah)

All of this is dhikr.

We can increase the amount of dhikr we do by simply doing the tasbīh mentioned above at different times of the day. For example, on our daily commutes, whilst travelling, when waiting for something such as a doctor's appointment, while carrying out chores, or in any spare moment we get.

THE REMEMBRANCE OF ALLAH ENCOMPASSES (CONT):

Doing good and staying away from sins for the sake for the sake of Allah

→ Doing good deeds, be it salāh, charity, cooking, earning for the family, visiting the ill, forgiving others, etc. while seeking Allah's pleasure, beseeching Him to accept it from us, and giving us the tawfīq to do more good deeds.

→ Staying away from committing all kinds of sins, major or minor, solely for the sake of Allah.

All of these acts will help us have constant remembrance of Allah.

Remembering Allah by the tongue is a commendable act, but what is better than that is when the servant remembers Allah at the time of his sinning, and then due to that remembrance of Allah stops himself from sinning.

The Prophet (ﷺ) said:

"By Allah, Allah is more pleased with the repentance of His servant than what one of you would do on finding a lost camel in the waterless desert. When he draws near Me by the span of his hand, I draw near him by the length of a cubit; and when he draws near Me by the length of a cubit, I draw near him by the length of a fathom; and when he draws near Me walking, I draw close to him hurriedly." (Sahīh al-Muslim)

ii To obey Him and never disobey Him

One who gives the haqq of taqwa to Allah is one who:

Obeys Allah Almighty:	By completing the obligatory acts like prayer, fasting, maintaining ties of kinship, eating from the halāl and tayyib (pure), etc.
Never disobeys Him:	By avoiding sins like shirk, lying, disobeying parents (except in matters against Allah's obedience), backbiting etc.

We should strive against Shaytān and our nafs to live a life of obedience to Allah, as opposed to a life of disobedience. We pray in the manner Allah has taught us to pray through the Prophet (ﷺ) and not in the way of our forefathers or what we deem as right; we fast when instructed to fast and abstain from it when told to refrain, even during illness; we eat halāl and pure food, even when traveling to non-Muslim countries; we avoid ribā and earn a halāl earning, living within our means, etc.

iii To be grateful and never ungrateful

a. Grateful when bestowed with blessings

We must be grateful to Allah Almighty for all the great favors and blessings that He has bestowed on us in both the spiritual and worldly terms. None is deserving of both praise and thanks simultaneously and perpetually except Allah alone. Allah says:

وَمَا بِكُم مِّن نِّعْمَةٍ فَمِنَ ٱللَّهِ ﴿٥٣﴾

"And whatever blessings you have are from Allah."
(Sūrah an-Nahl, 16:53)

Being grateful is not just uttering al-hamdulillāh by the tongue. Rather, gratitude includes the involvement of the heart, tongue, as well as the physical faculties.

Ibn al-Qayyim (ﷺ) said:

"Gratitude may be in the heart, in submission and humility; on the tongue, in praise and acknowledgement; and in the physical faculties, by means of obedience and submission (i.e., keeping oneself away from committing sins and acts of disobedience that Allah has forbidden)." (Madārij as-Sālikīn)

Gratitude of the tongue

This involves constantly praising Allah with our tongue for our blessings. Recounting His favors upon us and our own failure to express sufficient gratitude for them will help us remain steadfast in continuously keeping the tongue moist with *'Alhamdulillāh'*.

Gratitude of the heart

This alludes to having constant recognition of Allah's blessings in our lives, thus humbling our ***nafs*** to His obedience even if it goes against our desires.

Gratitude of the physical faculties

This refers to making use of every blessing in a manner pleasing to Allah and keeping oneself away from committing sins and acts of disobedience that Allah has forbidden.

For instance, take the blessing of hair. How can we express gratitude for it and earn Allah's pleasure by it, apart from acknowledging it in the heart and saying - 'alhamdulillāh' with the tongue?

Maintaining its health and condition would be one of the primary ways we can show gratitude for the blessing of our hair. This is, in fact, an important aspect of the sunnah of Prophet Muhammad (ﷺ). He said,

"Whoever has hair, let him look after it properly." (Sahīh al-Bukhari)

Some ways we can take care of our hair is by washing it once a week; brushing or combing it to keep it tidy; starting to comb from the right side, followed by the left; coloring the white hair, preferably with henna tint; improving our dietary habits; and sleeping well.

What better way to earn Allah's pleasure than by doing such acts in adherence to the sunnah of our Prophet (ﷺ)?

b. Grateful when faced with trials

This is a very high level of gratitude. With a little effort, it is easy to be grateful constantly for the blessings that Allah has given us. But how can one be grateful when faced with trials? Trials that can be from a wide range of tests, such as:

- Death of a dear one
- Theft of wealth
- Sickness or physical ailment
- An abusive marriage where the woman's family won't let her divorce
- A neglectful marriage where the man doesn't have the means to remarry
- Critical illness of one's child
- Parents needing full-time care, but the adult child doesn't have the means to care for them

In these strenuous situations, responding with acceptance and patience is most definitely a difficult task, and most of us would be in a state of panic, complaining, and showing discontent.

In order to be grateful in such burdensome conditions:

→ We need to keep in mind, both blessings and calamities are from Allah, the All-Wise. Allah loves us much more than our own mother and if He has tested us with it, there is definitely some blessing in it.

→ We need to think good of Allah and look for the benefits in the adversity instead of focusing on the negative. Perhaps through these calamities, Allah is protecting us from a bigger harm, or He is expiating our sins, or elevating our ranks—all of which may not have been possible otherwise.

Take for instance, the story of Umm Salamah (رضي الله عنها). After reverting to Islam, she faced severe persecution from the Quraysh, due to which she migrated to Abyssinia. She set out with her husband, Abu Salamah, leaving behind her home and traveling to a new land, solely seeking the pleasure and reward of Allah. When they heard that Quraysh had eased the persecution on the Muslims, they decided to return to Mecca. However, on returning they realized that the Makkan persecution had only worsened. So, they decided to migrate again, but this time to Madinah with their baby. Sadly, Umm Salamah was not only prevented from migrating with her family, but she was also separated from her husband, and her child was snatched away from her. Imagine the grief and loneliness she would have felt then. When she was finally allowed to migrate with her child and join her husband, he had passed away. She sincerely loved her husband and believed there could be no better man than him. Despite all these trials, instead of despair, she grasped onto the rope of Allah even stronger to relieve her pain.

And how did Allah reward her for her patience? What did she get in exchange for the loss of her husband at the most critical juncture of her life? Marriage to the best of men, the Prophet Muhammad (ﷺ), and the status of being the 'mother of the believers'.

Ibn al-Qayyim (رحمه الله) says, "To be grateful when a calamity befalls us is superior to mere acceptance. In this case, the individual sees the calamity as a blessing, so he gives thanks to the One who is testing him for that test." ('Iddat as-Sābirīn)

9.1.4 Practical implications

What do we do if we find it difficult to obey certain commands of Allah or leave certain sins? How can we practically and systematically deal with the shortcomings in our 'ibādah? Here are two such examples with their possible solutions:

Example 1: Difficulty in praying five times a day

We must make a habit of praying the five daily prayers on time every day by taking baby steps towards it. Just as babies learn to walk by first crawling, then standing, and many, at times, stumbling, before they actually begin to take balanced steps forward, we need to take one little step at a time until we reach our goal. If, for example, we don't have a routine of praying at all, then we can start with praying once a day.

When babies fall, they don't give up. They continue trying, taking support to find balance. In the same manner, we must take all the support we can for our 'ibādah journey. Here's a sample of the 'baby steps' we can take.

Begin with making goals:

Action → **DIFFICULTY IN PRAYING FIVE TIMES A DAY**

Goal Setting

Week 1: Start praying one salāh in the day on time, at a time which will not be challenging.
If we mess up, we must make up the prayer as soon as we can. When we achieve the week's goal, we may treat ourselves with something we love, like a favorite chocolate cake. And if we fail to reach our goal, we can penalize ourselves, perhaps by forcing ourselves to stay away from social media or by deleting WhatsApp on the day we missed our prayer.

Week 2: Start praying three salāhs on time.
Building a habit often needs support. We can request someone to text or check with us about our prayers. Or we can use an app on our phone to remind us of our prayers.

Week 3 and beyond: Once praying three times a day becomes a routine, we can start praying all five salāhs on time.
This is a real achievement.

No matter how many years of salāh we may have missed, we must keep going. We should never let Shaytān delude us into thinking, 'It's too late now', or 'It's going to be very difficult'. There will be times when we experience inexplicable closeness with our Creator, and other times when we may feel no 'spiritual boost'. The latter episodes are what we need to be wary of as they are prone to make us feel like it's not worth continuing. However, no amount of guilt or shame should make us even think of leaving our prayers. Praying is an obligation. Remember, we are trying to perform this action to the best of our ability, solely for Allah's sake.

The support we can make use of in this case is:

- Patience and persistence
- Recognizing the importance and benefits of salāh
- It will be the first thing people will be accounted for on the Day of Judgment. (Musnad Ahmad)
- The five daily obligatory prayers expiate sins committed in between them as long as major sins are avoided. (Sahīh Muslim)
- Learning to pray salāh the right way and understanding what we are reciting in our prayers.
- Realizing the fact that we need salāh, not vice versa; and that the opportunity to pray is a blessing.

Example 2 : Difficulty in avoiding backbiting

Action → **BACKBITING**

Things to do

Sincerely asking Allah to save us from this sin. Making du'a with desperation to Allah to enable us to control our tongue.

Whenever we feel tempted to say something against someone, we must quickly remind ourselves about what the Prophet (ﷺ) told us: **"Whoever covers (the sin of) a Muslim, Allah will cover him (his sin) in this world and in the Hereafter."** (Sunan Ibn Mājah)

Keeping in mind that we might be backbiting against someone whom Allah loves, and that Allah says:
"Whosoever shows enmity to a walī (friend) of Mine, then I have declared war against him." (Sahīh al-Bukhari)

9.2 Levels of taqwa

According to Ibn al-Qayyim (ﷺ), taqwa has three levels:

The first: Protecting the heart and limbs from sins and all forbidden matters.

The second: Protecting the heart and limbs from disliked (makrūh) matters.

The third: Protecting oneself from fudūl (curiosity) and what does not concern him.

He (ﷺ) says, "The first gives the servant his life; the second gives him health and strength; and the third enables him to gain happiness, contentment, and light." (Al-Fawaa'id)

9.3 How can we manifest taqwa in our daily lives?

Taqwa manifests in several forms.

Adding to the list of examples mentioned in an article by Sr. Hina Mukhtar, here are some of the many ways taqwa materializes in our lives:

- The uneasy feeling that we get when we miss an obligation
- Feeling miserable about lying to someone
- Staying away from backbiting even when we are tempted to give in
- Giving up arguing even if we are in the right
- Holding back from taunting or mocking others for fear of accountability
- Avoiding hurting those whom we are angry or jealous of with our utterances or actions
- The guilt that follows when we hurt someone knowingly or unknowingly

- The shame and regret that follows a sin we've committed, knowing full well of its standing in the sight of Allah
- Finding it difficult to fall sleep the whole night after disobeying or disrespecting our parents
- Crying in the depths of the night, fearing none but the One above the Throne
- The fear that restricts us from sinning even when we are alone and nobody is looking
- The will to please Allah, even when the whole world is bent on displeasing Him
- Deciding to grow the beard or wear the hijāb for the sole reason of pleasing our Rabb
- Fulfilling one's promises even if that means we would incur loss
- The struggle to better ourselves according to Islam with each passing day

Taqwa is not about slipping but rising up again and never letting go. We need to prepare for the Hereafter, and the best provision on this journey of ours is to have taqwa (consciousness of Allah).

وَتَزَوَّدُواْ فَإِنَّ خَيْرَ ٱلزَّادِ ٱلتَّقْوَىٰۖ وَٱتَّقُونِ يَـٰٓأُوْلِي ٱلْأَلْبَـٰبِ ﴿١٩٧﴾

"And take a provision (with you) for the journey, but the best provision is taqwa (piety, righteousness, etc.). So fear Me, Oh men of understanding!"
(Sūrah al-Baqarah, 2:197)

9.4 How can we attain taqwa?

9.4.1 Keep in mind the benefits Allah has promised for those who adopt taqwa

Adopting taqwa may be a challenging task but its benefits are magnanimous. Perhaps if we learn about them, we'd find it easier to exercise taqwa. Allah, the Most Appreciate has guaranteed the following rewards in the Quran for those who adopt taqwa:

- Gaining Allah's love

بَلَىٰ مَنْ أَوْفَىٰ بِعَهْدِهِۦ وَٱتَّقَىٰ فَإِنَّ ٱللَّهَ يُحِبُّ ٱلْمُتَّقِينَ ٧٦

"Yes, whoever fulfils his pledge and fears Allah much; verily, then Allah loves those who are muttaqīn." (Sūrah Āli-'Imrān, 3:76)

- Guidance

ذَٰلِكَ ٱلْكِتَٰبُ لَا رَيْبَ ۛ فِيهِ ۛ هُدًى لِّلْمُتَّقِينَ ٢

"This is the Book (the Quran), whereof there is no doubt, a guidance for those who are muttaqīn." (Sūrah al-Baqarah, 2:2)

- Ease in matters

وَمَن يَتَّقِ ٱللَّهَ يَجْعَل لَّهُۥ مِنْ أَمْرِهِۦ يُسْرًا ٤

"And whosoever has taqwa of Allah and keeps his duty to Him, He will make for him ease in his matter." (Sūrah at-Talaq, 65:4)

- A way out of problems and difficulties

وَمَن يَتَّقِ ٱللَّهَ يَجْعَل لَّهُۥ مَخْرَجًا ٢

"And whosoever has taqwa of Allah and keeps his duty to Him, He will make a way for him to get out (from every difficulty)." (Sūrah at-Talaq, 65:2)

- Acceptance of deeds

إِنَّمَا يَتَقَبَّلُ ٱللَّهُ مِنَ ٱلْمُتَّقِينَ ٢٧

"Verily, Allah accepts only from those who are muttaqīn." (Sūrah al-Mā'idah, 5:27)

⦿ Unexpected sustenance

وَلَوْ أَنَّ أَهْلَ ٱلْقُرَىٰٓ ءَامَنُوا۟ وَٱتَّقَوْا۟ لَفَتَحْنَا عَلَيْهِم بَرَكَـٰتٍ

مِّنَ ٱلسَّمَآءِ وَٱلْأَرْضِ وَلَـٰكِن كَذَّبُوا۟ فَأَخَذْنَـٰهُم بِمَا كَانُوا۟ يَكْسِبُونَ ﴿٩٦﴾

"And if the people of the towns had believed and had taqwa, certainly, We should have opened for them blessings from the heaven and the earth, but they belied (the Messengers). So We took them (with punishment) for what they used to earn."
(Sūrah al-'Araf , 7:96)

⦿ Salvation from the Hellfire

ثُمَّ نُنَجِّى ٱلَّذِينَ ٱتَّقَوا۟ وَّنَذَرُ ٱلظَّـٰلِمِينَ فِيهَا جِثِيًّا ﴿٧٢﴾

"Then We shall save those who had taqwa. And We shall leave the wrongdoers therein (humbled) to their knees (in Hell)."
(Sūrah Maryam, 19:72)

⦿ Ability to distinguish truth from falsehood

يَا أَيُّهَا الَّذِينَ آمَنُوا إِن تَتَّقُوا اللَّهَ يَجْعَل لَّكُمْ فُرْقَانًا

وَيُكَفِّرْ عَنكُمْ سَيِّئَاتِكُمْ وَيَغْفِرْ لَكُمْ وَاللَّهُ ذُو الْفَضْلِ الْعَظِيمِ ﴿٢٩﴾

"Oh you who believe! If you obey and have taqwa of Allah, He will grant you a criterion and will expiate for you your sins, and forgive you, and Allah is the Owner of the great bounty."
(Sūrah al-Anfal, 8:29)

⦿ Forgiveness of sins

يَا أَيُّهَا الَّذِينَ آمَنُوا إِن تَتَّقُوا اللَّهَ يَجْعَل لَّكُمْ فُرْقَانًا

وَيُكَفِّرْ عَنكُمْ سَيِّئَاتِكُمْ وَيَغْفِرْ لَكُمْ وَاللَّهُ ذُو الْفَضْلِ الْعَظِيمِ ﴿٢٩﴾

"Oh you who believe! If you obey and have taqwa of Allah, He will grant you a criterion and will expiate for you your sins, and forgive you, and Allah is the Owner of the great bounty."
(Sūrah al-Anfal, 8:29)

⊙ Success

وَٱتَّقُواْ ٱللَّهَ لَعَلَّكُمۡ تُفۡلِحُونَ ٢٠٠

"...have taqwa of Allah, so that you might succeed."
(Sūrah Āli-'Imrān, 3:200)

9.4.2 Accepting the guidance of the Quran

Allah, the All-Wise, has sent down the Quran for our guidance. If we live according to its teachings, Allah will increase us further in guidance and grant us tawfīq of taqwa.

وَٱلَّذِينَ ٱهۡتَدَوۡاْ زَادَهُمۡ هُدٗى وَءَاتَىٰهُمۡ تَقۡوَىٰهُمۡ ١٧

"As for those who accept guidance, He (Allah) increases their guidance and bestows on them their taqwa."
(Sūrah Muhammad, 47:17)

A few examples of guidance from the Quran which we can live by, so that we will qualify for more guidance and taqwa include:

Examples	Quranic Reference
Avoid saying a word of disrespect to parents	"Say not to them (so much as) "uff," and do not repel them but speak to them a noble word." (Sūrah al-Isrā', 17:23)
Restrain anger	"Who spend (in the cause of Allah) during ease and hardship and who restrain anger and who pardon the people – and Allah loves the doers of good." (Sūrah Āli-'Imrān, 3:134)
Forgive the mistakes of others	"Show forgiveness, enjoin what is good, and turn away from the ignorant." (Sūrah al-'Araf , 7:199)

Examples	Quranic Reference
Refrain from spying and backbiting	"And do not spy or backbite each other. Would one of you like to eat the flesh of his brother when dead? You would detest it. And fear Allah. Indeed, Allah is Accepter of repentance and Merciful." (Sūrah al-Hujurat, 49:12)
Spend in charity	"Believe in Allah and His Messenger and spend out of that in which He has made you successors. For those who have believed among you and spent, there will be a great reward." (Sūrah al-Hadid, 57:7)
Avoid excessiveness	"Oh Children of Adam, take your adornment at every masjid; and eat and drink, but be not excessive. Indeed, He likes not those who commit excess." (Sūrah al-'Araf , 7:31)
Keep striving	"And that there is not for man except that (good) for which he strives." (Sūrah an-Najm, 53:39)
Seek forgiveness of Allah	"And whatever good you put forward for yourselves, you will find it with Allah. It is better and greater in reward. And seek forgiveness of Allah. Indeed, Allah is Forgiving and Merciful." (Sūrah al-Muzzammil, 73:20)

9.4.3 Seeking Allah's help

Taqwa helps us curb our desires, but to attain it is an uphill road.

We need to constantly beseech Allah to help us live a life of taqwa.

اللَّهُمَّ آتِ نَفْسِي تَقْوَاهَا
وَزَكِّها أنْتَ خَيْرُ مَنْ زكَّاها اَنْتَ وَلِيُّهَا وَمَوْلاَهَا

Allahumma āti nafsī taqwāhā, wa zakkihā, anta khairu man zakkāhā, anta waliyyuhā wa mawlāhā

"Oh Allah! Grant my soul its piety and purify it; You are the best to purify it. You are its Guardian and its Protecting Friend."
(Sahīh Muslim)

Chapter 10

Polish the Heart: The Seat of Taqwa

يَا مُقَلِّبَ الْقُلُوبِ ثَبِّتْ قَلْبِى عَلَى دِينِكَ

Oh turner of the hearts (Allah, the Most High), keep our hearts firm on your religion. (Silsilāh as-Sahīha)

After exploring the benefits of adopting taqwa from the Quran in the previous chapter, let us look at yet another reward promised by Allah for the muttaqīn—Paradise. Imagine the beautiful picture Allah is painting for us in the following āyah so as to encourage us to adopt taqwa, rather than follow our lusts and desires.

مَّثَلُ ٱلْجَنَّةِ ٱلَّتِى وُعِدَ ٱلْمُتَّقُونَ ۖ فِيهَآ أَنْهَٰرٌ مِّن مَّآءٍ غَيْرِ ءَاسِنٍ وَأَنْهَٰرٌ مِّن لَّبَنٍ لَّمْ يَتَغَيَّرْ طَعْمُهُۥ
وَأَنْهَٰرٌ مِّنْ خَمْرٍ لَّذَّةٍ لِّلشَّٰرِبِينَ وَأَنْهَٰرٌ مِّنْ عَسَلٍ مُّصَفًّى ۖ وَلَهُمْ فِيهَا مِن كُلِّ ٱلثَّمَرَٰتِ وَمَغْفِرَةٌ مِّن
رَّبِّهِمْ ۖ كَمَنْ هُوَ خَٰلِدٌ فِى ٱلنَّارِ وَسُقُوا۟ مَآءً حَمِيمًا فَقَطَّعَ أَمْعَآءَهُمْ ﴿١٥﴾

"The description of Paradise which the muttaqun have been promised is that in it are rivers of water, unaltered; rivers of milk that never changes in taste; rivers of wine delicious to those who drink; and rivers of clarified honey (clear and pure). Therein for them is every kind of fruit, and forgiveness from their Lord. (Are they) like those who shall dwell forever in the Fire, and be given to drink, boiling water, so that it cuts up their insides?"
(Sūrah Muhammad, 47:15)

Taqwa is all about what lies in the heart. The actions of our heart are actually the feelings that emerge before we do any action—be it sincerity, love, tawakkul (trust in Allah), inābah (turning to Allah with repentance), hope, fear, reverence, awe, or contentment.

The Prophet (ﷺ) said,

"...taqwa is here," and he pointed to his heart three times. (Sahīh Muslim)

If our heart is filled with taqwa, our limbs will automatically follow with righteous actions. In addition, when a Muslim rectifies his heart with purifying actions, such as good deeds, sincerity, truthfulness, and love for Allah and His Messenger, his limbs will turn upright as stated in the following hadīth:

"Indeed, within the body is a morsel of flesh; if it is sound, then the whole body will be sound and if it is corrupt, then the whole body will be corrupt. Indeed, it is the heart." (Sahīh al-Bukhari)

This hadīth contains the greatest indication that the rectification of our external activities (via our limbs) is directly connected to the rectification of our internal activities (via our heart and soul).

"If the heart is good and in it is only the desire of pleasing Allah and of that which He desires from us, the limbs will only proceed towards that which Allah desires. Consequently, the limbs hasten towards that which incurs the pleasure of Allah, and refrain from what Allah dislikes or what is feared that would be disliked by Allah even if it is not sure of that." (Jāmi' al-'Ulūm wal-hikam)

This is in sharp contrast to a corrupt heart which is conquered by a love for desires, which chases lusts, and places the wants of the nafs above everything else. Consequently, the external activities of a person in such a plight, will all be corrupt.

Depending on whether the heart is filled with the longing for success in the Hereafter or that of this fleeting worldly life, the limbs will strive accordingly.

Therefore, it is imperative upon us to rectify and beautify our hearts before adorning our outward actions. Enhancing the apparent deeds whilst the inner state is corrupt is like decorating a dirty, cluttered house with flowers and candles. Its beautification will be temporary and ineffective. So, just as we need to first cleanse our house, de-clutter it, and then work on its beautification, so too should we work on cleansing our hearts from sins first before concentrating on beautifying it.

Allah is all-knowing of what is inside our chests just as He is ever-watching of our external behavior. He knows what we hate, what we love, what we reject, and what we oppose. His focus is on our hearts, not on our bank account or looks, as the Prophet (ﷺ) said,

"Verily, Allah does not look at your appearance or wealth; rather He looks at your hearts and actions." (Sahīh Muslim)

10.1 Types of hearts

A heart that is soft	A heart that is hard
The land of this heart is soft, it absorbs the 'water' of knowledge and advice and causes its owner to reform and become righteous. We can plough it, dig it, and sow a seed inside it. Then, over time it will grow and produce fruits benefiting others as well.	The land of this heart does not absorb any goodness. Rather it rejects it and brings about no rectification for the Hereafter. We cannot plough it, dig it nor sow a seed. Therefore, it will neither benefit itself not others. Such a heart is corrupt.

As a result, it is essential for us to soften our hearts by purifying and beautifying them, constantly watering them with knowledge and removing the weeds of shirk, hypocrisy, jealously, and greed that corrupt them, and by continually protecting them from their predators—Shaytān and the nafs. With righteous actions, the heart can keep flourishing and blooming, and ultimately attain Allah's pleasure. This is tazkiyah.

Allah says, **"He who purifies it will indeed be successful." (Sūrah ash-Shams, 91:9)**

Ibn Kathir says in his 'Book of Tafsīr', explaining the above verse:

"(This refers to) he who purifies his soul through obeying Allah and who purifies it from the sins and immoral manners. Self-purification is about clearing out all the sordid tarnishing of the baser self with all its ugliness and evil and adding in all the good morals and noblest manners."

10.2 How to purify the nafs?

Thus, as mentioned in chapter 5, tazkiyah is a two-way process which includes cleaning and removing the sins of the heart, everything bad and evil,and adorning the heart with righteous good deeds, everything noble and high.

10.2.1 Cleaning and removing the sins of the heart

Knowledge

We need to learn to recognize the sicknesses of our heart (intangible dirt) before we start the cleaning process.

Observation

To gauge and measure how dirty or clean our heart is, we need to look out for signs of a hardening heart by observing the actions of our limbs and tongue. Our outwards actions will indicate the purity of our heart.

The scholars say we suffer from a hardened heart if we feel that we have one or more of the symptoms below:

(i) Lacking consciousness of Allah.

One who lacks consciousness of Allah is heedless and negligent towards their duties towards Allah—be it worshipping Him alone, praying salāh, giving zakāh, or enjoying good and forbidding evil, etc.

(ii) Unable to taste the sweetness of faith

Acts of worship have sweetness when performed. But one with a hardened heart cannot taste this sweetness. Rather, for them, worship becomes more of a routine or, even worse, a burden.

(iii) Being untouched by the verses of the Quran

A hardened heart is neither able to take lessons from the Quran, nor able to shed tears out of fear when hearing about the punishments of the Hereafter and the torments of Hell. The Quranic verses regarding warning have no impact on it.

(iv) Indifference to advice

One with a hardened heart becomes indifferent to any advice given to them, especially if it goes against their lowly desires. Even if it is of extreme benefit, it falls on deaf ears.

10.2.2 Implementing 'cleaning tools'

The hardening of the heart is such a powerful and dangerous disease that Allah Almighty actually uses it as a punishment for people, as a hardened heart is far away from receiving His pleasure.

فَبِمَا نَقْضِهِم مِّيثَٰقَهُمْ لَعَنَّٰهُمْ وَجَعَلْنَا قُلُوبَهُمْ قَٰسِيَةً ۖ ﴿١٣﴾

"So because of their breach of their covenant, We cursed them, and made their hearts grow hard..." (Sūrah al-Mā'idah, 5:13)

In order to clean the heart and remove unwanted dirt and illnesses from it, such as shirk, hypocrisy, jealousy, arrogance, hatred, greed, and other impurities, we will need effective tools.

10.3 Tools to clean the heart

10.3.1 Knowledge of Allah

The more we know Allah, the more we will love and fear Him; and this will help prevent us from doing wrong out of shyness from Him.

Ibn Rajab (ﷺ) says:

"...the heart cannot be rectified unless there settles within it, knowledge of Allah, His greatness, love of Him, fear and awe of Him, hope and tawakkul in Him, and for it to be overflowing with this. This is the reality of tawhīd and the meaning of 'none has the right to be worshipped except Allah'."

Here are a few examples of how the knowledge of Allah will help us rectify our heart:

KNOWLEDGE	RESULT
Allah is the Ever Living who never dies.	**Result:** We do everything for His sake alone. **Heart is purified from:** Shirk, kufr, hypocrisy.
Allah alone is our Creator, Protector, Provider, only Guardian, and He alone causes life and death. Only He operates this entire universe.	**Result:** We completely trust in Allah and ask Him alone. **Heart is purified from:** Jealousy and greed.

Allah is the Almighty, severe in punishment. People will be punished as a result of that which they used to do. If people wrong one another, they will experience some of its retribution in this world also.

→

Result:
We will not behave unjustly towards others, nor will we retaliate with more than what is fair.
Heart is purified from:
Hatred and feelings of vengeance.

Allah says in a hadīth qudsī:
"O My slaves, I have forbidden injustice for Myself and forbade it for you also. So avoid being unjust to one another."
(Sahīh Muslim)

10.3.2 Inābah ilAllah (Returning to Allah)

The heart hardens with disobedience. The more sins one commits, the harder the heart becomes, and the tougher it will be to cleanse it. A hardened heart is weak and is easily attracted by the whispers of Shaytān, our blatant enemy. The solution to this would be to repent immediately and make du'a for guidance.

"Verily, when the servant commits a sin, a black spot appears upon his heart. If he abandons the sin, seeks forgiveness, and repents, then his heart will be polished. If he returns to the sin, the blackness will be increased until it overcomes his heart." (Sunan at-Tirmidhī)

Tawbah opens doors of mercy but it requires sincerity, owning our faults, and giving up the wrong as well.

إِنَّ ٱللَّهَ يُحِبُّ ٱلتَّوَّٰبِينَ وَيُحِبُّ ٱلْمُتَطَهِّرِينَ ﴿٢٢٢﴾

"...Indeed, Allah loves those who are constantly repentant and loves those who purify themselves."
(Sūrah al-Baqarah, 2:222)

Allah doesn't say "Allah accepts" but says "Allah loves..." those who are constantly repentant. How beautiful and powerful is that! Tawbah essentially means insisting on going back to Allah, and Allah loves it when we insist on going back to Him.

So, if we're in a position of making tawbah, then we are in a position of receiving the love of Allah. Isn't it evident now as to why Shaytān wants us to feel hopeless and prevents us from seeking forgiveness and tawbah?

His ultimate goal is to divert us from the path of Allah. Tawbah not only puts us back on track, but also earns us the love of Allah Almighty, the Most Merciful, Most Loving, and Most Affectionate.

It is very important that we do not expose our sins, especially if the Almighty has concealed them:

"All of my ummah (nation of followers) will be excused, except for the mujāhirīn (those who make their sins known). And verily it is a kind of mujāharah (exposing one's sins) that a man does something (sinful) at night, and then in the morning, when Allah has screened his sin for him, he says, 'Hey, so-and-so! I did such-and-such last night...'. And the night passed with his Lord screening him, and he wakes up casting aside the screen of Allah from himself." (Sahīh Muslim)

10.3.3 Ways to rely upon Allah

⊙ Abandoning three things

Sheikh ibn Uthaymeen (ﷺ) states,

From the things to reform the heart are:

→ Leaving what doesn't concern you

→ Leaving arguments which have no benefit

→ Leaving causing separation between people

10.3.4 Feeding the poor and patting the orphans

The Prophet (ﷺ) said,

"If you want to soften your heart, feed the poor and pat the head of the orphan." (Musnad Ahmad)

10.3.5 Avoid talking too much

The Prophet (ﷺ) said,

"Do not speak too much without mentioning Allah. Verily, talking too much without remembering Allah hardens the heart. The furthest of people from Allah is one with a hard heart." (Sunan at-Tirmidhī)

10.3.6 Remembrance of Allah

أَلَا بِذِكْرِ ٱللَّهِ تَطْمَئِنُّ ٱلْقُلُوبُ ﴿٢٨﴾

"Verily, in the remembrance of Allah do hearts find rest."
(Sūrah ar-Ra'd, 13:28)

Our heart will be happy and at peace depending on the extent of our remembrance of Allah. Allah's remembrance, as mentioned before, includes total dependence upon Him, turning to Him for aid, having good thoughts about Him, and waiting for victory from Him, besides supplications and adhkār.

"There is hardness in the heart that is not melted away except with the remembrance of Allah, the Most High. Therefore, it is befitting for the worshipper to treat the hardness of his heart with the remembrance of Allah." (al-Wābil as-Sayyib)

10.3.7 Prioritizing the love of Allah Almighty and His Prophet (ﷺ) over all other love

The ability to love is implanted within us by our Merciful Lord. So, it is natural to love our family, our wealth, and our land, but our biggest love must be reserved for Allah and His Prophet (ﷺ). Rather, this is what Allah has commanded us to do.

قُلْ إِن كَانَ ءَابَآؤُكُمْ وَأَبْنَآؤُكُمْ وَإِخْوَٰنُكُمْ وَأَزْوَٰجُكُمْ وَعَشِيرَتُكُمْ
وَأَمْوَٰلٌ ٱقْتَرَفْتُمُوهَا وَتِجَٰرَةٌ تَخْشَوْنَ كَسَادَهَا وَمَسَٰكِنُ تَرْضَوْنَهَآ أَحَبَّ إِلَيْكُم
مِّنَ ٱللَّهِ وَرَسُولِهِۦ وَجِهَادٍ فِى سَبِيلِهِۦ فَتَرَبَّصُوا۟ حَتَّىٰ يَأْتِىَ ٱللَّهُ بِأَمْرِهِۦ ۗ
وَٱللَّهُ لَا يَهْدِى ٱلْقَوْمَ ٱلْفَٰسِقِينَ ﴿٢٤﴾

"Say (Oh Prophet), 'If it be that your fathers, your sons, your brothers, your mates, or your kindred; the wealth that you have gained; the commerce in which you fear a decline; or the dwellings in which you delight, are dearer to you than Allah, or His Messenger, or the striving in His cause; then wait until Allah brings about His decision. And Allah guides not the rebellious.'" (Sūrah at-Tawbah, 9:24)

Our heart is created for loving Allah Almighty. We should not tear it apart by searching for love, security, or perfection from other than Allah because of the following reasons:

⊙ Our heart will not find peace and security nor be at rest except by loving Allah Almighty.

⊙ By loving others besides Allah, we will inevitably be let down because no human being is perfect; everyone has their fair share of faults and weaknesses.

10.4 Supplications advised by the Prophet (ﷺ)

A sound and healthy heart serves as an emotional bank for storing and retrieving good feelings and helps build a positive mindset. It provides an upright station for our intentions, as the heart is the permanent residence of all intentions. Above all, a pure heart results in a nafs that has a sound spiritual perception and that which helps us lead a simple lifestyle while using our resources wisely.

In order to get help in the journey of tazkiyah and taste the sweetness of eemān, we need to beseech Allah through the supplications our Prophet (ﷺ) has taught us:

Guide your heart

اللَّهُمَّ اهْدِ قَلْبِي وَسَدِّدْ لِسَانِي وَاسْلُلْ سَخِيمَةَ قَلْبِي

Allahumma-hdi qalbī wa saddid lisānī wa-slul sakhīmata qalbī

"Oh Allah guide my heart, correct my tongue, and remove the malice from my heart."

(Sunan Abī Dāwūd)

Fill it with light

اللَّهُمَّ اجْعَلْ فِي قَلْبِي نُورًا

Allāhumma-j'al fī qalbī nūran

"Oh Allah make (for me) a light in my heart."

(Sahīh al-Bukhari)

Make it firm

يَا مُقَلِّبَ الْقُلُوبِ ثَبِّتْ قَلْبِي عَلَى دِينِكَ

Ya muqalliba-l-qulūbi thabbit qalbī 'alā dīnika

"Oh Allah, the turner of the hearts, make my heart firm on Your religion.""

(Sunan at-Tirmidhī)

Cleanse it

اللَّهُمَّ اغْسِلْ قَلْبِي بِمَاءِ الثَّلْجِ وَالْبَرَدِ وَنَقِّ قَلْبِي مِنَ الْخَطَايَا كَمَا نَقَّيْتَ الثَّوْبَ الْأَبْيَضَ مِنَ الدَّنَسِ

Allahumma-ghsil qalbī bi mā'i-th-thalji wal-baradi wa naqqi qalbī minal-khatāyā kamā naqqaita-th-thawba-l-abyada mina-d-danasi

"Oh Allah! Wash my heart with the water of snow and hail, and cleanse my heart from all sins as a white garment is cleansed from filth."

(Sahīh al-Bukhari)

Protect it

رَبَّنَا لَا تُزِغْ قُلُوبَنَا بَعْدَ إِذْ هَدَيْتَنَا وَهَبْ لَنَا مِن لَّدُنكَ رَحْمَةً إِنَّكَ أَنتَ الْوَهَّابُ

Rabbanā lā tuzigh qulūbanā b'ada idh hadaitanā wa hab lanā min-ladunka rahmatan innaka anta-l-Wahhāb

"Our Lord, let not our hearts deviate after You have guided us and grant us from Yourself mercy. Indeed, You are the Bestower."

(Sūrah Āli-'Imrān, 3:8)

Make it sound

وَأَسْأَلُكَ قَلْبًا سَلِيمًا وَلِسَانًا صَادِقًا

Wa as'aluka qalban salīman wa lisānan sādiqan

"And I ask You for a sound heart and a truthful tongue."

(Sunan an-Nasā'ī)

Adorn it

اللَّهُمَّ حَبِّبْ إِلَيْنَا الْإِيمَانَ وَزَيِّنْهُ فِي قُلُوبِنَا

Allahumma habbib ilaina-l-eemāna wa zayyinhu fī qulūbinā

"Oh Allah, make us love belief
and adorn our hearts with it."

(al-Adab al-Mufrad)

Cool it down

اللَّهُمَّ بَرِّدْ قَلْبِي بِالثَّلْجِ وَالْبَرَدِ وَالْمَاءِ الْبَارِدِ اللَّهُمَّ نَقِّ قَلْبِي مِنَ الْخَطَايَا كَمَا نَقَّيْتَ الثَّوْبَ الأَبْيَضَ مِنَ الدَّنَسِ

Allahumma barrid qalbī bith-thalji wal-baradi wal-mā'i-l-bāridi; Allahumma naqqi qalbī minal-khatāyā kamā naqqaita-th-thawba-l-abyada mina-d-danasi

"Oh Allah, cool my heart with snow, hail, and cold water. Oh Allah, cleanse my heart of sins as You cleanse a white garment of filth."

(Sunan at-Tirmidhī)

There are different levels of purification that bring us closer to Allah. Reciting the Quran and performing good deeds polishes our hearts and cleanse our sins from sins. However, for some sins to be wiped out, repentance or expiation through trials is first required. Moreover, some sins may have penetrated deeply, thus purifying them would need a deeper sense of cleaning - just as strong stains on our clothes require what we call 'cold cleaning'. That is why, according to scholars, we are taught to ask Allah to cool our hearts with a 'deep cleansing' from the hard-stained sins, so that we don't end up suffering their consequences or going through tough trials for their expiation.

Sins cause burning desires. We ask Allah to cool these burning desires for us, and to help us neither long for sins nor commit them. We ask Allah to never let us be in the proximity of sins, and to distance us from them with a distance like that between the East and the West.

After purifying our heart from sins, we ask Allah, the Most Merciful, to adorn our hearts with faith.

The Prophet (ﷺ) said,

"Verily, Allah has vessels among the people of the earth, and the vessels of your Lord are the hearts of his righteous servants. The most beloved of them to Him are the softest and the most tenderest of them." (Musnad al-Shāmīyyīn)

We need to ask ourselves:

→ What is the state of my heart? Is it soft, or hardened?

→ Can I resist sins or do I keep returning to them?

→ If given a choice, would I click on a YouTube lecture about Islamic knowledge, or would I click on a video of the life of a superstar?

→ When was the last time I picked up the Quran to recite, understand, and live by it?

→ Has my seeking of knowledge been reduced to just watching a few minutes of lectures, or am I regular with studying beneficial courses?

→ When was the last time I checked to see how many times I disobeyed my Lord whilst looking down on non-Muslims for their disobedience?

→ Am I spreading the treasures of Islam to benefit others just as I have benefitted tremendously because of the efforts of our Salaf?

Granted, we cannot be at a state of spiritual high all the time, but we can however make the effort to frequently polish our hearts because only when the heart is good does the rest of the body follow in goodness.

May Allah Almighty guide us to adopt means that will soften our hearts and stay away from those things that harden our hearts so that we may be amongst those who are the most beloved to Him.

Aameen.

Chapter 11

True Essence of Living

اللَّهُمَّ إِنِّي أَسْأَلُكَ بِرَحْمَتِكَ الَّتِي
وَسِعَتْ كُلَّ شَيْءٍ، أَنْ تَغْفِرَ لِي

Oh Allah, I ask You by Your mercy, which
encompasses all things, that You forgive me.
(Sunan Ibn Mājah)

After creating humankind, Allah didn't leave us without a purpose. He made it clear that we were created to worship Him alone and He took a covenant from us that we will fulfil this purpose.

وَإِذْ أَخَذَ رَبُّكَ مِنۢ بَنِىٓ ءَادَمَ مِن ظُهُورِهِمْ ذُرِّيَّتَهُمْ
وَأَشْهَدَهُمْ عَلَىٰٓ أَنفُسِهِمْ أَلَسْتُ بِرَبِّكُمْ ۖ قَالُوا۟ بَلَىٰ ۛ شَهِدْنَآ ۛ
أَن تَقُولُوا۟ يَوْمَ ٱلْقِيَـٰمَةِ إِنَّا كُنَّا عَنْ هَـٰذَا غَـٰفِلِينَ ﴿١٧٢﴾

"And (remember) when your Lord brought forth from the Children of Adam, from their loins (or from Adam's loin, his offspring) and made them testify as to themselves (saying), 'Am I not your Lord?' They said, 'Yes! We testify,' lest you should say on the Day of Resurrection, 'Verily, we have been unaware of this.'"
(Sūrah al-'Araf , 7:172)

We have no excuse to shun this covenant now. In fact, we must strive to fulfil it with ihsān.

To experience the true essence of living we must:

11.1 Purify our intentions

11.2 Have ihsān

11.3 Adopt zuhd

11.1 Purifying our intentions (niyyah)

Before we initiate anything, we need to check our intentions and perform a true self-assessment.

Why are we performing the action (even if the action in question were a smile)?	What is the motive behind this action?

→ Is it for the sake of Allah Almighty or seeking people's praise to become famous?

→ Is our focus on Allah or other people?

→ Are we wanting Allah's pleasure or the pleasure of others?

→ Do we expect reward from Allah alone or from people, whether it be gratitude and acknowledgement or any tangible reward.

Self-assessment, to 'stop and think', before doing any act is not easy. But the realization of the fact that acceptance of our deeds depends upon our intentions will encourage us to keep check on them before doing any act. We don't want the fruits of our efforts and the opportunity to earn reward to be wasted.

The Prophet (ﷺ) said,

"Actions are according to intentions, and everyone will get

what was intended" (Sahīh al-Bukhari).

11.1.2 What will help us in purifying our intentions?

When we know that:

⊙ Allah is All-Knowing and knows the true intentions behind our actions, we will be Allah-and-Hereafter centric instead of people-and-world centric.

⊙ He, The All-Seer, is seeing that we are trying our best, we will not worry about results. We will continue our efforts against all odds and try our utmost best.

⊙ He alone will reward us for it. It will enable us to remove people from the picture and continue doing good, irrespective of whether people reciprocate what we did for them or not.

Ibn al-Qayyim (ﷺ) said:

"The heart will rest and feel relief if it is settled with Allah. And it will worry and feel anxious if it is settled with the people." (Al-Fawaa'id)

'What people think' is one of the biggest trials of life that we burden ourselves with because trying to satisfy others is a never -ending struggle. Worrying about what people will think of us is futile because of the following reasons:

- They will never be truly pleased with us. And even in the cases they genuinely are, their pleasure will be short-lived.

- They can neither benefit nor harm us without the permission of Allah.

In such a case, is it worth proving ourselves to anyone other than Allah? We will be setting ourselves up for failure, disappointment, and misery if we give power to the creation. It is only when we become true slaves of Allah, only concerned about what He thinks of us and our actions, will we free ourselves from being a slave to people's opinions.

We need to detach ourselves from all that causes us to drift away from the remembrance of Allah Almighty.

11.2 What is ihsān?

The Prophet (ﷺ) was asked,
"Oh Allah's Messenger, what is ihsān?" He (ﷺ) said,
"Ihsān is to worship Allah as if you see Him, and if you do not achieve this state of ibādah, then (take it for granted that) Allah sees you."
(Sahīh al-Bukhari, Sahīh Muslim)

Let us take the recitation of the Quran, for example. One could merely recite the Quran and attain its due rewards. But ihsān when reciting the Quran would be to perform the wudu', find oneself a quiet and secluded place, recite the glorious words of Allah Almighty in a beautiful and slow tone, paying utmost attention with absolute awe and humility to every single word and every single phrase which is being recited so that one's heart would soften, one's eyes would become wet, one's skin would tremble with the fear of Allah, and one would want to spontaneously bow down in prostration unto their Lord. That then would be the degree of ihsān when reciting the Glorious Quran whereby one can see his Lord, or at least know and believe with total and absolute conviction that his Lord Almighty can and does see Him. (IslamHelpline.Net)

We are in a state of 'ibādah whenever we fulfil all that pleases Allah and stay away from all that displeases Him. Worship is not only a set of rituals, like praying, fasting, performing hajj, or giving zakāh, it is beyond that. Rather, it is living a life of servitude in every aspect of our life. The way we walk, the way we eat, what we eat, what we wear, what we watch, what we hear, our sleeping and waking-up, our entertainment, our friends, where we hang out, matters of marriage, divorce, inheritance, relationships - our whole code of life should be in accordance with how Allah wants us to live.

Servitude also embodies how we deal with our finances, morals, and ethics. If we are in a state of servitude, we cannot deal in or with what is harām, we cannot cheat people, do whatever we please, or deal with His creation in whichever way we wish - be it with humans, animals, or the environment. Islam shows us the wholesome way of life, the true essence of living, which comprises of:

Being conscious of Allah Almighty at all times, in every walk of life - be it in our business of running a shop or managing people or in our dealings with our spouse, children, friends, neighbors, and society.

Dedicating all our actions and utterances to Him alone, out of love for Him, hoping for His mercy and fearing His wrath.

Getting our heart attached to Allah alone.

11.3 Zuhd (detachment)

Attachment is a feeling of love and strong connection that emerges from the heart. When we attach our heart to anything besides Allah, be it a person or a thing, it will weigh us down and weaken our faith, hence leading to our own debasement and ruin. To avoid this, we need to detach from everything and everyone besides Allah. This is what is called 'zuhd' (detachment) in Islam.

Detachment doesn't mean withdrawal from the world and whatever is in it. It does not imply we cannot own and enjoy the luxuries of this world. Rather, what it implies is that we can own things without letting them own or control us. It is not the rejection of the favors of Allah, rather it is the rejection of the heart's attachment to them. Even though we are permitted to fully enjoy whatever lawful pleasure Allah has bestowed on us, our ultimate attachment should be with Him alone, the True Provider, if we truly believe in His Words:

وَمَا هَٰذِهِ ٱلْحَيَوٰةُ ٱلدُّنْيَآ إِلَّا لَهْوٌ وَلَعِبٌ

وَإِنَّ ٱلدَّارَ ٱلْءَاخِرَةَ لَهِىَ ٱلْحَيَوَانُ لَوْ كَانُوا۟ يَعْلَمُونَ ﴿٦٤﴾

"What is the life of this world but amusement and play? But verily the home in the Hereafter - that is life indeed, if they but knew."
(Sūrah al-'Ankabūt , 29:64)

From the parable below we see how low a value Allah has placed for this world.

It was narrated that Sahl ibn Sa'd said:

"We were with the Messenger of Allah (ﷺ) in Dhul-hulaifah, when we saw a dead sheep lifting its leg (because of bloating). He (ﷺ) said: 'Don't you think this is worthless to its owner? By the One in whose hand is my soul, this world is more worthless to Allah than this (dead sheep) is to its owner. If this world was worth the wing of a mosquito to Allah, the disbeliever would not have a drop to drink from it.'" (Sunan Ibn Mājah)

Notice how vividly our Prophet (ﷺ) has showed us the true picture of this world.

Allah has placed us in this world as a test, and to facilitate our journey towards the Hereafter. We must use it as a means to continue on our path to Allah and not make it our final destination. The wise thing for us to do would be to use our life on this earth as a means to achieve our ultimate purpose - Allah's pleasure and His paradise. Mindful detachment will help us focus on this end goal.

Allah Almighty teaches us detachment through different obligations He has prescribed on us. Take, for instance:

Salāh

Our five obligatory prayers (salāh), where we are expected to leave everything we are involved in solely to have an exclusive connection with Allah - be it our household chores, the job we're performing, our studying for an upcoming test, or the project we can't get off our mind.

Fasting

Fasting, which is a detachment from food, drink, sexual intimacy, and vain speech to uplift our spiritual self and gain closeness to Allah alone.

Zakah

Zakāh (charity), which is all about detaching ourselves from our wealth and giving portions of it away for the sake of Allah.

With a change of mindset and intention, we can make the most of this world to earn our Hereafter.

11.4 What are the rewards and benefits mentioned in the Quran for the remembrance of Allah?

Allah's remembrance is one of the greatest ways to fulfil our purpose in this life - to worship the Almighty by submitting to Him, obeying Him, and loving Him. Allah bestows incredible and uncountable rewards for those who engage in His remembrance.

To enlist a few:

Success

Allah Almighty says:

وَاذْكُرُوا اللّٰهَ كَثِيرًا لَّعَلَّكُمْ تُفْلِحُونَ

"...and remember Allah much that you may be successful."

(Sūrah al-Anfal, 8:45)

Forgiveness and Paradise

Allah Almighty says:

وَٱلذَّٰكِرِينَ ٱللَّهَ كَثِيرًا وَٱلذَّٰكِرَٰتِ أَعَدَّ ٱللَّهُ لَهُم مَّغْفِرَةً وَأَجْرًا عَظِيمًا

"...and (for) men and women who remember Allah much, Allah has prepared for them forgiveness and a great reward."

(Sūrah al-Ahzāb, 33:35)

Allah's companionship and closeness

The Prophet (ﷺ) told us that Allah Almighty has said: "I am with My servant when he remembers Me and his lips move making mention of Me." (Sahīh al-Bukhari)

Raising your status

The Prophet (ﷺ) said, "Should I not inform you of the best of your deeds, the most sanctifying of them before your Lord, and which does more to raise your status with Him. (A deed) that is better for you than the disbursement of gold and money or battle with the enemy whereby you strike at their necks and they strike at yours?"
The Companions said, "What is it, O Messenger of Allah?"
He (ﷺ) replied, "Remembrance of Allah."

(Musnad Ahmad, Sunan Ibn Mājah)

Peace and mercy from Allah

The Prophet (ﷺ) said,
"People will not sit remembering Allah without the angels surrounding them, mercy covering them, peace descending on them, and Allah mentioning them among those who are with them." (Sahīh Muslim)

A solution for depression and anxiety

Allah says in the Quran:

أَلَا بِذِكْرِ ٱللَّهِ تَطْمَئِنُّ ٱلْقُلُوبُ

"Verily, in the remembrance of Allah do hearts find rest."
(Sūrah ar-Ra'd, 13:28)

Relief from Shaytān

The Prophet (ﷺ) said,
"The devil is encircling the heart of the son of Adam. When he mentions Allah, he withdraws; but when he is neglectful, he makes evil suggestions." (Sahīh al-Bukhari)

11.5 What does remembrance of Allah comprise of?

As discussed earlier, remembrance of Allah is an all-embracing term and is not restricted to certain rituals or acts of worship. Prayers, zakāh, fasting, and hajj are the practical manifestations of remembering Allah. Moreover, the remembrance of Allah is not confined to the tongue and actions of the limbs but includes our heart, mind, and process of thinking. It involves thinking of and making mention of Allah at all times and in every area of our lives. This is the worship that has no particular or specified time but is performed constantly such that it permanently connects one's life to Allah and His servitude.

ٱلَّذِينَ يَذْكُرُونَ ٱللَّهَ قِيَـٰمًا وَقُعُودًا وَعَلَىٰ جُنُوبِهِمْ ﴿١٩١﴾

"(They are) those who remember Allah, standing, sitting, and lying on their sides..." (Sūrah Āli-'Imrān, 3:191)

We should strive to be amongst such people. The more we practice dhikr the more we will want to do it because righteous deeds open doors to more good deeds.

11.5.1 Learning Allah's names and attributes, and living by them

This form of dhikr is par excellence. The constant awareness of Allah's names and attributes manifesting around us works as a solution to all our problems. In addition, asking by His names and attributes will amplify our supplications. Allah Almighty commands us to supplicate to Him by invoking His beautiful names.

وَلِلَّهِ ٱلْأَسْمَآءُ ٱلْحُسْنَىٰ فَٱدْعُوهُ بِهَا ۖ وَذَرُوا۟ ٱلَّذِينَ يُلْحِدُونَ فِىٓ أَسْمَـٰٓئِهِۦ ۚ
سَيُجْزَوْنَ مَا كَانُوا۟ يَعْمَلُونَ ﴿١٨٠﴾

"And Allah's names are the best names, so call on Him and leave those who violate the sanctity of His names. They shall be recompensed for what they did." (Sūrah al-'Araf , 7:180)

Whenever we wish for anything, however big or small, there is a name that is suitable for it. For instance:

- For provisions to keep us self-sufficient, we can ask by Allah's name, Ar-Razzāq, the Provider.
- To help us overcome the difficulties in our daily life, we can beseech Al-Muhaymin, the Overseer.
- To seek forgiveness, we must turn to Al-Ghaffār, the All-Forgiving.
- For precious gifts, including support and refuge, we can ask by Allah's name, Al-Karīm, the Most Generous, the One who continually bestows us with the grandest of bounties even though we may not

be deserving of it.

- When we are unable to get the desired results, we must remember Al-Basīr, the One who is able to see all matters however small or minute, whether hidden or apparent. We must tell ourselves not to worry about the results and continue to put in our best efforts.

Prophet Muhammad (ﷺ) said,

"Allah loves that when you engage in some work, you do so with proficiency." (Sunan al-Baihaqī)

This will encourage and inspire us to carry out our tasks with sincerity as we believe Al-Basīr is seeing our actions.

- When we're lost or drowned in the darkness of our sins, we ask An-Nūr to grant us from His Nūr (light), to guide us and remove us from darkness towards light.

Know that Allah Almighty grants in abundance. His treasures are never-ending and never-diminishing. He can grant us all that we desire and more. If we were to ask for an ounce of gold, He is fully able to give us a mountain of it. We should never shy away from asking Him with full conviction, and never lose patience if our du'as are delayed.

11.5.2 Make everyday situations a means to remembering Allah

Remembrance of Allah plants the tree of faith in the heart. It nourishes and develops it thereafter. The more we increase in the remembrance of Allah, the stronger our faith will become. So, we should benefit from every situation by remembering Allah Almighty.

Here are a few examples where mundane instances can be utilized to remember Allah:

- When we hear good news, we could take just a few seconds to thank Allah for what he has blessed us with.

- When we feel apprehensive about something and wish to calm our nerves, we can glorify Allah and remember that He is capable over everything.

▸ When our hunger, thirst or other necessities are taken care of, we can have our hearts rush to Allah in gratitude.

▸ When hurt by people, we can resort to crying and complaining to Allah alone.

▸ When unsure which path to take in life, instead of losing heart, we must have hope in Allah, while begging for His help and taking the first step required to pursue our goals.

11.5.3 Remembrance of Allah in our day to day routine

Our Prophet (ﷺ) has taught us the appropriate supplications for every occasion. Making an effort to learn them and consciously applying them in our day-to-day routines will amount to our remembrance and worship of Allah and will become a source of barakah in everything we do. To mention a few combination of Adhkār:

Getting up in the morning

الْحَمْدُ لِلَّهِ الَّذِي أَحْيَانَا بَعْدَ مَا أَمَاتَنَا وَإِلَيْهِ النُّشُورُ

Alhamdu lillahi-lladhi ahyāna b'ada mā amātanā wa ilaihi-n-nushūr

(All praise is for Allah who gave us life after having taken it from us and unto Him is the resurrection.)

Retiring to bed

بِاسْمِكَ اللَّهُمَّ أَمُوْتُ وَأَحْيَا

BismikAllahumma amūtu wa ahyā

(In Your name Oh Allah, I live and die.)

Starting to do any task

بِسْمِ اللّٰهِ

Bismillah

(In the name of Allah.)

At the time of eating

The Prophet (ﷺ) said,
"When you are about to eat, you should say:

بِسْمِ اللَّهِ

Bismillah (In the name of Allah)

...and if you forget to say it before starting, then you should say (when you remember):

بِسْمِ اللَّهِ فِي أَوَّلِه وَآخِرِهِ

Bismillāhi fī awwalihi wa ākhirihi (In the name of Allah in its beginning and end)."

Before entering the toilet

(بِسْمِ اللَّه) اللَّهُمَّ إِنِّي أَعوذُ بِكَ مِنَ الْخُبْثِ وَالْخَبائِثُ

(Bismillah) Allāhumma innī a'ūdhubika min-al-khubthi wal-khabā'ith

[(In the name of Allah.) Oh Allah, I take refuge with you from all temptations of male and female demons.]

Leaving the house

بِسْمِ اللَّهِ، تَوَكَّلْتُ عَلى اللَّهِ وَلا حَوْلَ وَلا قُوَّةَ إِلاّ بِاللَّه

Bismillāhi tawakkaltu 'alAllāhi wa la hawla wa la quwwata Illa billāh

(In the name of Allah, I place my trust in Allah, and there is no might nor power except with Allah.)

Entering marketplaces

لا إِلهَ إِلاّ اللَّه وحدَهُ لا شريكَ لهُ، لهُ المُلْكُ ولهُ الحَمْد، يُحْيي
وَيُميتُ وَهُوَ حَيٌّ لا يَموت، بِيَدِهِ الْخَيْرُ وَهوَ على كلّ شيءٍ قدير

Lā ilāha illAllāhu wahdahu la sharīka lahu, lahul-mulku wa lahu-hamdu, yuhyī wa yumītu wa huwa hayyun la yamūtu, bi yadihi-l-khairu wa huwa 'alā kulli shay'in qadīr

(None has the right to be worshipped except Allah, alone, without partner, to Him belongs all sovereignty and praise. He gives life and causes death, and He is living and does not die. In His hand is all good and He is over all things, omnipotent.)

Du'a and adhkār in the mornings and evenings

The morning and evening adhkār and many more are available in the book, Hisnul Muslim (also known as 'Fortress of the Muslim'), which is widely available at bookshops and stores. These supplications are also available on digital applications which can be downloaded onto our phones and referred to at any time of the day.

Chapter 12

The Winning Strategies

رَبَّنَا عَلَيْكَ تَوَكَّلْنَا وَإِلَيْكَ أَنَبْنَا وَإِلَيْكَ الْمَصِيرُ

Our Lord! In You we have placed our trust,
and to You we turn in repentance,
and to You is the final return.
(Sūrah al-Mumtahanah, 60:4)

The desires of our nafs and the whispers of Shaytān make our remembrance and worship of Allah, in its true essence, difficult to do. Overcoming them becomes a constant struggle.

We must observe how Allah beautifully consoles His slaves in their difficulties.

We can take any story of the previous nations as an example and see whether it was Allah:

⊙ Inspiring Musa's mother to put her baby in the basket and throw it into the sea, or

⊙ Commanding Musa (عليه السلام) to take hold of the frightening snake, or

⊙ Confront the intimidating Pharoah.

One recurring consolation of Allah was: "FEAR NOT"

قَالَ خُذْهَا وَلَا تَخَفْ ۖ سَنُعِيدُهَا سِيرَتَهَا ٱلْأُولَىٰ ﴿٢١﴾

"Allah said: 'Grasp it, and fear not,
We shall return it to its former state.'"
(Sūrah Ta-Ha, 20:21)

This is the concept we need to embody within our lives: fear not. And the reason why we should not fear or be scared is not because of our physical strength, our manpower, or any other worldly reason. Rather, it should be our trust in Allah.

12.1 Tawakkul (trust)

Trust is the one thing that will help us navigate our lives towards our purpose and maintain our sanity despite the constant assaults from these two enemies of ours. We are not alone. Rather, Allah is there for us, and He is sufficient to help, guide, and protect us.

وَٱللَّهُ أَعْلَمُ بِأَعْدَآئِكُمْ ۚ وَكَفَىٰ بِٱللَّهِ وَلِيًّا وَكَفَىٰ بِٱللَّهِ نَصِيرًا ﴿٤٥﴾

"Allah has full knowledge of your enemies, and Allah is sufficient as a walī (protector), and Allah is sufficient as a helper."
(Sūrah an-Nisā', 4:45)

With each new daunting attack, it helps to know that Allah, the Most Loving, is certainly with us, guiding us. Our duty is to live up to the challenges we may face in this life fearlessly - not because of our own capabilities or the means in front of us, but because of the strong conviction that Allah is with us. He guides us to what is best, and His plans are always the best ones for us.

12.2 Examples from Musa's life (عليه السلام) on how having trust in Allah can work wonders

Example 1:

When we look at it, Musa (عليه السلام) was one of the strongest men. Yet, Allah Almighty did not command him to not have fear because of his strength. Rather, He Almighty commanded him (عليه السلام) not to fear because Allah Almighty was with him.

Example 2:

Likewise, when Pharoah and his armies were right behind Musa (عليه السلام) and his followers, pursuing them to kill them, and Allah inspired Musa (عليه السلام) to strike the sea with his staff as a solution, there was a genuine reason to be petrified. That was why the Children of Israel said, "We are sure to be overtaken (by Pharoah and his army, we are scared)." But how did Musa (عليه السلام) respond? He said, "No, indeed my Rabb is with me and He will guide me."

فَلَمَّا تَرَٰٓءَا ٱلْجَمْعَانِ قَالَ أَصْحَٰبُ مُوسَىٰٓ إِنَّا لَمُدْرَكُونَ ﴿٦١﴾

قَالَ كَلَّآ ۖ إِنَّ مَعِىَ رَبِّى سَيَهْدِينِ ﴿٦٢﴾

"And when the two hosts saw each other, the companions of Musa (Moses) said: 'We are sure to be overtaken.' (Musa) said: 'Nay, verily! With me is my Lord, He will guide me.'"
(Sūrah ash-Shu'arā, 26:61-62)

So when Musa (عليه السلام) struck the sea with his staff, Allah made it split into two gigantic mountains of waves on either side. Just the feeblest of means was enough to accomplish this enormous task of splitting the sea. This shows us that it is all about trusting Allah first and then exerting efforts from our side. The results are always from Allah, according to His wisdom.

The onus of fulfilling our demanding tasks and roles is on us. This is because in Paradise, ranks are based on our deeds, and on how we played our role in the world. This necessitates that we identify our roles and fulfil it to the best of our ability, asking Allah for tawfīq as He is the only One who will grant us the means, capabilities, and opportunities to fulfil our roles and achieve our goals in the best of manners.

اللَّهُمَّ رَحْمَتَكَ أَرْجُو فَلا تَكِلْنِي إِلَى نَفْسِي طَرْفَةَ عَيْنٍ

وَ أَصْلِحْ لِي شَأْنِي كُلَّهُ ، لا إِلَهَ إِلَّا أَنْتَ

Allāhumma rahmataka arjū falā takilnī ilā nafsī tarfata 'ayn, wa aslihī sha'nī kullahu, lā ilāha illa anta

(Oh Allah, I hope for Your Mercy. Do not leave me to myself even for the blinking of an eye. Correct all of my affairs for me. There is none worthy of worship but You.)
(Sunan Abu Dawūd)

We need to ask ourselves: How am I playing the roles I've been given - as a spouse, parent, in-law, sibling, boss, employee, etc.? Am I fulfilling my roles with ihsān, regardless of how they treat me, or am I basing all of my behavior on how they are with me?

We are not perfect so we should not expect perfection from others either. No matter how they behave with us - whether good or bad - we will not be questioned about their behavior. But we will be questioned about how we behave and respond to them. We will be called to account if we reciprocate with rudeness and malice and rewarded if we fulfill our duty towards them at a level of ihsān. We must learn to forgive them and move on and to not take things personally. Rather, we must strive to see Allah's nurturing behind all of it.

Allah, At-Tawwāb, accepts the repentance of the sinners and forgives their sins. On the same token, Al-'Adl, the Most Just, punishes those who deserve punishment.

12.3 Quick strategies to achieve nafs al-Mutma'innah

We have to fulfil the purpose of our creation - being upright upon obedience to Allah Almighty, guarding His commands, and refraining from His prohibitions - in order to achieve success with Him. We have to unceasingly work on the purity of our heart so as to meet Allah Almighty with nafs al-Mutma'innah. We can do this by, first and foremost, asking Allah to help us overcome the hindrances from our nafs and Shaytān.

Allah Almighty has power over everything. He humiliates whoever He wishes and elevates whoever He wishes. He gives honor to whoever He wishes and disgraces whoever He wishes. He is just. He is extremely tolerant and forbearing, and He values and rewards service and worship rendered to Him.

By believing in these facts about Allah...

Our focus will be to please Allah alone, not people.

We will not fear facing challenges because we know "Allah is with us and He will guide us."

We will strive to be close to Allah Almighty by sincerely returning to Him alone with our hearts, mind and ***nafs***.

As Ibn al-Qayyim (ﷺ) said:

"Let's strive to be close to Allah. Let's long for the dwelling of peace wherein there is no toil, stress, or weariness." (Al-Fawaa'id)

This can be achieved by the following the beneficial recommendations:

by Imām ibn – Qayyim al-Jawzīyyah ..

→ **The heart**, returning to Allah almighty with love, supplication, humiliation and brokenness.

→ **The mind** returning by action upon the commands of the loved One, surrendering to them, and giving them authority over all else – for there remains in the mind no doubt or suspicion about them.

→ **The *nafs*** returning by obediently following the commands, and by giving up lowly habits, immoral behavior, and corrupt intentions. Instead, it completely follows His commands, surrendering to Him and wanting Him over everything else.

→ **The *nafs*** no longer contains desires that challenge Allah Almighty's command, and it authorizes its Rabb in managing its affairs. It surrenders to His rule, while being content with His decree.

(Tarīq al-hijratain wa bāb as-aa'ādatain)

For these pious ones Allah almighty will address:

"O nafs al-Mutma'innah (The Tranquil Self)
Come back to your Lord, well-pleased (yourself)
And well-pleasing unto Him! Enter you, then, among
My honored slaves,and enter you My Paradise!"
(Sūrah Al-Fajr, 89:27-30)

May Allah make us from them!

Shortcut to Protection: Du'as

اللّهُمَّ عالِمَ الغَيْبِ وَالشّهادَةِ فاطِرَ السّماواتِ وَالأرْضِ
رَبَّ كلِّ شَيءٍ وَمَليكَه ، أَشْهَدُ أَنْ لا إِلهَ إِلاّ أَنْت
أَعوذُ بِكَ مِن شَرِّ نَفْسي وَمِن شَرِّ الشَّيْطانِ وَشِرْكِه
وَأَنْ أَقْتَرِفَ عَلى نَفْسي سوءاً أَوْ أَجُرَّهُ إِلى مُسْلِم

Allāhumma 'alimal-ghaibi wash-shahadati, fatiras-samawati wal-ardhi, Rabba kulli shai'in wa maleekahu. Ash-hadu an la ilāha illa anta, a'oodhu bika min sharri nafsi, wa min sharrish-shaitani wa shirkihi, wa an aqtarifa 'alaa nafsi soo'an aw ajurrahu ila muslim

(Oh Allah! Creator of the heavens and the earth, Knower of the hidden and the exposed, Rabb of everything and everyone. I bear witness that none has the right to be worshipped but You. I seek Your Protection from the evil of my own self, from the evil of Shaytān, and from the evil of shirk to which he calls, and from bringing evil to myself or to another Muslim.) (Sunan Abu Dawūd, Sunan at-Tirmidhī)

Commenting on this supplication, Ibn al-Qayyim (ﷺ) said,

"The Prophet (ﷺ) mentioned the two sources of evil: the self (nafs) and Shaytān. He also mentioned the two victims of evil: one's own self or his Muslim brother. Hence, this hadīth has combined the sources of evil, its causes, and where it leads in the briefest yet clearest and most comprehensive expression." (Badā'i' al-Fawā'id)

The Prophet (ﷺ) said,

"(Reciting) Sūrah al-Ikhlaas and the mu'awwidhatayn (i.e., Sūrah al-Falaq and Sūrah an-Nās) three times in the morning and three times in the evening will suffice you in all respects." (Sunan Abu Dawūd)

He (ﷺ) also said about the mu'awwidhatayn that "people have never sought refuge by means of anything like them." (Sunan an-Nasā'ī)

Appendix

Assalāmu 'alaikum,

I am delighted that you chose to read this book. I pray to Allah that you benefit through its lessons and insights.

Here, I would like to make a few requests:

a) If you found this book useful, please share it with your family and friends and suggest it to others.

b) Please leave a review of this book on Amazon and Goodreads.

c) For constructive criticism and/or feedback you may reach me at thabaatpublications@gmail.com

d) For information on our upcoming books and/or to benefit from our blog, please visit our website www.thabaatpublications.com

Whatever good is from Allah alone, and whatever evil is from myself and Shaytān.

JazākumAllāhu khair,

Your sister,

Umm Muhammad

Other books by the author

When the Two Seas Meet: Building Bonds
"Navigating a Mother-in-law's Internal Struggle"

The Beauty of Time Management in Islam

Upcoming books

Journey from Salty Sea to Sweet
Excelling in the Role of Daughter-in-law

References

1. Abdul-Wahid, A.K. (2018). Twenty Ways to Avoid the Places, Conduct and Plots of Shaytān (Ruqyah Series, Part 1) [online] Abukhadeejah.com. Available at: http://www.abukhadeejah.com/20-ways-to-avoid-the-places-conduct-and-plots-of-Shaytān-ruqyah-series-1 (Accessed: Oct. 2020).

2. AbdurRahman.org. (2011). Meaning of the Āyah "...and follow not the footsteps of Shaitan" – Permanent Committee. [online] AbdurRahman.org. Available at: https://abdurrahman.org/2011/09/02/meaning-of-the-āyah-and-follow-not-the-footsteps-of-shaitan/ (Accessed: Oct. 2020).

3. IslamQA.info. (2020). Beware of the Whispers of the Shaytān about Allah. [online] Available at: https://islamqa.info/en/answers/98295/beware-of-the-whispers-of-the-Shaytān-about-allah. (Accessed: Oct. 2020).

4. Mogahed, Y. (2019). Beware. [online] Islamic Reminders. Available at: https://www.facebook.com/permalink.php?story_fbid=2762262813801023&id=228598547167475 (Accessed: Oct. 2020).

5. AbdurRahman.org. (2018) Shaytaan is a Strong External Reason which causes Eemaan to Decrease – Shaykh 'Abdur-Razzaak al-'Abbaad [online] AbdurRahman.org. Available at: https://abdurrahman.org/2018/09/06/shaytaan-a-strong-external-reason-which-causes-eemaan-to-decrease/ (Accessed: Oct. 2020).

6. IslamQA.info (2010). Whispers from the Shaytaan – Islam Question & Answer. [online] Available at: https://islamqa.info/en/answers/21052/whispers-from-the-shaytaan. (Accessed: Oct. 2020).

7. AbdurRahman.org (2018). Exerting Efforts Towards Accomplishing

Sincere Righteous Actions: One of the causes for the increase of eemaan – Shaykh 'Abdur-Razzaak al-'Abbaad. [online] AbdurRahman.org. Available at: https://abdurrahman.org/2018/11/25/exerting-efforts-towards-accomplishing-sincere-righteous-actions/ (Accessed: Nov. 2020).

8. Elias, A.A. (2017). Hadīth on Prayer: What if you are unsure how much you prayed? [online] Daily Hadīth Online. Available at: https://www.abuaminaelias.com/dailyhadīthonline/2017/11/09/what-unsure-how-much-prayed/ (Accessed: Nov. 2020).

9. Elias, A. A. (2019). Hadīth on women: Among greatest trials for men is women. [online] Daily Hadīth Online. Available at: https://www.abuaminaelias.com/dailyhadīthonline/2017/10/23/greatest-fitnah-men-women/ (Accessed: Nov. 2020).

10. Elias, A.A. (2021). Daily Hadīth Online. [online] Available at: https://www.abuaminaelias.com/dailyhadīthonline/ (Accessed: Sept. 2020).

11. Faris, M. (n.d.). The Productive Muslim Guide to Beating Procrastination. [online] Available at: https://productivemuslim.com/procrastination (Accessed: 26 Dec. 2020).

12. Farooq, A.H.M. (2018). The Whispers of Satan – Its Reasons and Its Role and Its Remedies. [online] The Salafi Masjid. Available at: https://www.wrightstreetmosque.com/the-whispers-of-satan-its-reasons-and-its-role-and-its-remedies/ (Accessed: Dec. 2020).

13. Edota, A. (2014). Winning Against Your Nafs. [online] Youthly Hub. Available at: http://youthlyhub.com/winning-nafs/ (Accessed: Jan. 2021).

14. IslamicBoard.com. (2009). Hope in Allah (subanna wa ta'ala). [online] Available at: https://www.islamicboard.com/manners-and-purification-of-the-soul/134281251-hope-allah-subanna-wa-ta-ala.html. (Accessed: Jan. 2021).

15. Mukhtar, H. (2019). Taqwa. [online] Medium. Available at: https://medium.com/@shsuperior786/taqwa-658f50d3bc63 (Accessed: Feb. 2021).

16. Islamhelpline.net. (n.d.). What is ehsan ahsan. [online] Available at: http://islamhelpline.net/answer/7946/what-is-ehsan-ahsan (Accessed: Feb. 2021).

17. Al-Jawzīyyah, I. Q. Badaa-I' al-Fawaa-id.

18. Al-Qayyim, I. Al-Fawaa'id.

19. Al-Qayyim, I. Ad-Daa wad-Dawaee (Al-Jawab Al-Kaafi).

20. Rajab, I. Jāmi' al-'Ulūm wal-hikam.

Glossary

'ibādah.....acts of worship
adhān.....call to prayer
akhlaaq.....character (often, good)
alhamdulillah.....phrase which means 'All Praise is due to Allah'
al-khulafa' al-rāshidūn.....the four rightly-guided Caliphs
al-mu'awwidhatayn.....term given to the last two chapters of the Quran
amānah.....a trust
'aqīdah.....principles of one's belief in Allah
āyah.....a verse of the Quran
barakah .....blessings
bid'ah.....innovation in religion
d'awah.....invitation to Islam
dīn.....religion, a way of life
dhikr.....remembrance of Allah
du'a.....beseeching Allah for something of this world or the Hereafter
eemān.....faith
fahshā.....moral corruption; indecency; obscenity
Fajr.....prayer at dawn
fard.....obligatory
fiqh.....Islamic jurisprudence
fitrah.....natural inclination, innate predisposition
fudūl.....curiosity
hadīth.....narration of the final prophet, Muhammad (peace be upon him)
hadīth qudsīh.....saying of the Prophet (peace be upon him) whose meaning is revealed directly by Allah
hajj.....pilgrimage to Makkah
halāl.....lawful, permitted
haqq.....due right; also, truth
haram.....unlawful, prohibited

hijāb...Islamic dress code for women (and men)
ihsān...quality of excellence
ilāh...Deity worthy of worship
imām...leader
inābah...turning to Allah (in repentance and obedience)
iqāmah..second call to prayer, made immediately before the prayer
Isti'āda..seeking refuge with Allah against Satan
isti'anah ....seeking help of Allah
Istighfār ....asking Allah for forgiveness
istikhārah..seeking counsel from Allah for attaining good
istinshāq...cleaning the nostrils by inhaling water during ablution
istinthār..blowing water out of the nose during ablution
jabr...to compel, to force
jamā'ah...congregation
Jannah..Paradise
juz'..a part of the thirty in the Quran
khalīfah..vicegerent, successor
khalwah..seclusion with a person of the opposite gender who is lawful for marriage
kufr...disbelief in Allah
lamam...minor sin
makrūh...disliked
masjid...mosque
Mawlid...celebration of the Prophet's (peace be upon him) birthday
mu'amalāt..Islamic rulings governing commercial transactions
mubah..permissible
muhsinīn..those who do deeds to perfection, to the best of their ability
mujāharah...exposing one's sins
Mujāhidah...struggling towards good

mujāhirīn..those who commit sins openly or disclose their sins to people
muslimah..a Muslim female
muttaqīn..those who are conscious of Allah, God-fearing
nafs..inner disposition of a human being
nafs al-AmmārahBissu'.....................the commanding self
nafs al-Lawwāmah..............................the reproaching self
nafs al-Mutma'innah...........................the tranquil self
niyyah...intention
non-mahram.......................................those who are permissible to marry; observing hijāb (for women) in front of them is obligatory
Nūr..light
nutfah...mixed drops of male and female sexual discharge
qaylūlah...afternoon nap
Rabb...Lord, Allah
raka'āt..units of prayer
ribā...interest, usury
ruqyah shar'iyyah...............................remedies from the Sunnah
sabr...patience, tolerance, self-control
sadaqah..charity
sadaqah jaariyah................................ongoing charity, charity that continues to benefit even after one's death
salaf..pious predecessors
salāh...prayer
shayaTīn..devils
Shaytān..Satan
shirk..associating partners with Allah
sujūd as-sahw.....................................prostration of forgetfulness
sunnah...tradition of the Prophet (peace be upon him); also, supererogatory
Sūrah..chapter of the Quran
t'awīdh..amulet